CURRIES

CURRIES

160 AUTHENTIC RECIPES SHOWN IN 240 PHOTOGRAPHS

MRIDULA BALJEKAR

southwater

This edition is published by Southwater,
an imprint of Anness Publishing Ltd,
108 Great Russell Street, London WC1B 3NA;
info@anness.com

www.southwaterbooks.com;
www.annesspublishing.com

If you like the images in this book and would like
to investigate using them for publishing, promotions
or advertising, please visit our website
www.practicalpictures.com
for more information.

A CIP catalogue record for this book is available
from the British Library.

Publisher: Joanna Lorenz
Editor: Anne Hildyard
Designer: Nigel Partridge
Production Controller: Pirong Wang
Additional Recipes: Christine Ingram,
Manisha Kanani, Sally Mansfield, Sallie Morris
and Jennie Shapter
Photographers: Edward Allwright, David Armstrong,
Nicki Dowey, Amanda Heywood, Ferguson Hill,
Janine Hosegood, David Jordan, David King,
Patrick McLeavey and Sam Stowell

PUBLISHER'S NOTE
Although the advice and information in this book
are believed to be accurate and true at the time of
going to press, neither the authors nor the publisher
can accept any legal responsibility or liability for any
errors or omissions that may have been made nor
for any inaccuracies nor for any loss, harm or injury
that comes about from following instructions or
advice in this book.

NOTES
Bracketed terms are intended for
American readers.
For all recipes, quantities are given in both
metric and imperial measures and, where
appropriate, measures are also given in
standard cups and spoons. Follow one
set, but not a mixture, because they
are not interchangeable.
Standard spoon and cup measures are
level. 1 tsp = 5ml, 1 tbsp = 15ml,
1 cup = 250ml/8fl oz
Australian standard tablespoons are 20ml.
Australian readers should use 3 tsp
in place of 1 tbsp for measuring small
quantities. American pints are 16fl oz/
2 cups. American readers should use
20fl oz/2.5 cups in place of 1 pint when
measuring liquids.
Electric oven temperatures in this book are
for conventional ovens. When using a fan
oven, the temperature will probably need
to be reduced by about 10–20°C/20–40°F.
Since ovens vary, you should check with
your manufacturer's instruction book
for guidance.
The nutritional analysis given for each
recipe is calculated per portion (i.e. serving
or item), unless otherwise stated. If the
recipe gives a range, such as Serves 4–6,
then the nutritional analysis will be for the
smaller portion size, i.e. 6 servings. The
analysis does not include optional
ingredients, such as salt added to taste.
Medium eggs are used unless
otherwise stated.

Contents

Introduction

Spiced sauces or curries have been used for centuries to liven up rice, noodles, vegetables, meat and pulses. Although similar types of spices are used in curries worldwide, it is the preparation and the particular combination of spices that makes each dish unique.

CURRY GOES GLOBAL

India and countries in South-east Asia are important areas in the history of the spice trade and the wonderful curries they produce focus on careful blending of spices and the addition of chillies and fresh herbs. Curries are now popular worldwide, and there are many Indian, South-east Asian and other ethnic cafés and restaurants. However, it is easy to make authentic, delicious curries at home, and this book will show you how much fun it is to create unique and exciting curries in your own kitchen.

As well as providing exotic flavours, curries can be very healthy. Fresh fish and meat are served in small quantities with side dishes of fresh salads, curried vegetables, pickles, chutneys, yogurt, breads and boiled rice or noodles. Also, some of the ingredients used in curries have certain medicinal properties, for example garlic and fresh root ginger are renowned for their beneficial effects on the heart and stomach respectively.

SPICE MIXTURES

The most common spices used in curries are turmeric, cumin, coriander, mustard seeds, cardamom pods, ginger and chilli powder; when combined they add a wonderful zest, aroma and depth of flavour. Curries that are based on coconut milk and coconut cream in south India are very similar in character to those of South-east Asia. They are distinguishable because South Indian curries often use curry leaves, while South-east Asian dishes prefer kaffir lime leaves.

India has been influenced by many foreign cooking styles with the result that this endlessly versatile cuisine is multi-layered, dynamic and colourful.

BURMA TO BRAZIL

The whole world loves curry, and this book offers recipes that come from almost every continent. As well as popular classics from India such as Tandoori Chicken, Lamb Dhansak and

ABOVE: *This Cambodian chicken curry uses spices with the addition of fish sauce.*

ABOVE: *Samosas are crisp little pastries filled with spiced meat or vegetables.*

ABOVE: *Biryani is a dish based on basmati rice, with meat or vegetables added.*

Prawn Korma, look for Fiery Octopus, a very hot dish with gochujang chilli paste from Korea; Burmese Fish Stew, infused with lemon grass, ginger and fish sauce; or Spiced Cambodian Chicken Curry which has the tangy flavours of galangal, nuoc cham and garam masala. Lahore-style Lamb blends warm spices such as cinnamon, cloves and black peppercorns, while Ethiopian Curried Chicken is spiced with nutmeg, cardamom and paprika; Curry Kapitan with Coconut and Chilli Relish is fired with a tamarind, five-spice powder and shrimp paste to produce a fusion of Chinese, Malay, Portugese and Indian cuisines. Jungle Curry of Guinea Fowl from Thailand uses fresh green peppercorns and refreshing kaffir lime leaves. Chinese Duck Curry is a Thai recipe with the Chinese influences of five-spice powder and sesame oil, while an Israeli Aubergine Curry is fired up with very hot chillies and ras al hanout, a classic mixture which combines all the familiar spices, as well as fenugreek and fennel seeds.

USING THIS BOOK

Perfect for cooks who love preparing spicy food, this book provides a superb collection of 160 authentic curry recipes. With a choice of regional specialities from India, South-east Asia and many more countries around the world, popular classics and modern innovative recipes, the cook will have a huge source of ideas when cooking for the family, for entertaining or for special occasions. Most of the recipes serve four or six people but the quantities can be halved to serve two, or doubled up to serve eight people.

At the end of the book, a guide outlines the key spice ingredients, with hints, techniques and tips for storing foods, preparing them, making ahead of time, freezing, how to make your own curry powders and pastes, and also how to make perfect rice and a variety of breads.

Fish and Shellfish Curries

Fish has a delicate flavour, and lends itself to subtle spicing. This section offers a selection of spicy fish and shellfish curries from cuisines as varied as Burmese, Korean, Brazilian and Thai, as well as Indian. Thai curries are flavoured with chillies, lemon grass, coconut milk and kaffir lime leaves; Indian and Malayan curries use warm spices such as cinnamon, allspice and cumin to produce fragrant fish and shellfish curries.

White fish with light curry sauce

This combination of flavours also works well with other flat fish like turbot, halibut and brill. The spicing of this dish should be subtle or it will mask the delicate flavours, so use a mild curry powder.

Serves 4

4 white fish fillets, such as John Dory, each about 175g/6oz, skinned
15ml/1 tbsp sunflower oil
25g/1oz/2 tbsp butter
salt and ground black pepper
15ml/1 tbsp fresh coriander (cilantro) leaves and 1 mango, peeled and diced, to garnish

FOR THE CURRY SAUCE

30ml/2 tbsp sunflower oil
1 carrot, chopped
1 onion, chopped
1 celery stick, chopped
white of 1 leek, chopped
2 garlic cloves, crushed
50g/2oz creamed coconut, crumbled or 120ml/4fl oz/½ cup coconut cream
2 tomatoes, peeled, seeded and diced
2.5cm/1in piece fresh root ginger, grated
15ml/1 tbsp tomato purée (paste)
5–10ml/1–2 tsp mild curry powder
500ml/17fl oz/generous 2 cups chicken or fish stock

1 Make the sauce. Heat the oil in a pan; add the vegetables and garlic. Cook until soft but not brown.

2 Add the coconut, tomatoes and ginger. Cook for 1–2 minutes, stir in the tomato purée and curry powder. Add the stock, stir and season. Bring to the boil, lower the heat, cover and simmer for 50 minutes.

3 Allow the sauce to cool, then blend or process until smooth. Return to a clean pan and reheat gently. Adding a little water if too thick.

4 Season the fish fillets with salt and ground black pepper. Heat the oil in a large frying pan, add the butter and heat until sizzling. Carefully add the fish fillets and cook for about 2–3 minutes on each side, until pale golden and cooked through. Drain the fish on kitchen paper.

5 Arrange the fish fillets on plates, pour the curry sauce around the fish and sprinkle with the diced mango and coriander leaves. Serve with basmati rice.

Nutritional information per portion: Energy 333kcal/1391kJ; Protein 34.9g; Carbohydrate 12.5g, of which sugars 11.5g; Fat 16.3g, of which saturates 4.9g; Cholesterol 13mg; Calcium 102mg; Fibre 2.6g; Sodium 291mg.

Burmese fish stew

This tasty seafood curry originated in Burma but the mixture of complex spicing and creamy coconut milk has produced a dish that is also enticingly popular farther afield.

SERVES 8

675g/1¹/₂lb huss, cod or mackerel,
   cleaned but left on the bone
3 lemon grass stalks
2.5cm/1in piece fresh root ginger
30ml/2 tbsp fish sauce
3 onions, roughly chopped
4 garlic cloves, roughly chopped
2–3 fresh red chillies, seeded and chopped
5ml/1 tsp ground turmeric
75ml/5 tbsp groundnut (peanut) oil,
   for frying
400g/14oz can coconut milk
25g/1oz/¹/₄ cup rice flour
25g/1oz/¹/₄ cup gram flour
540g/1lb 5oz canned bamboo shoots,
   rinsed, drained and sliced
salt and ground black pepper
wedges of hard-boiled egg, thinly sliced
   red onions, chopped spring onions
   (scallions), deep-fried prawns (shrimp)
   and fried chillies, to garnish
rice noodles, to serve

1 Place the fish in a large pan and pour in cold water to cover. Bruise two lemon grass stalks and half the ginger and add to the pan. Bring to the boil, add the fish sauce and cook for 10 minutes. Lift out the fish and allow to cool. Strain the stock into a bowl. Discard any skin and bones and break the flesh into pieces.

2 Cut off the lower 5cm/2in of the remaining lemon grass stalk and discard; chop the remaining lemon grass. Place in a food processor or blender, with the remaining ginger, the onions, garlic, chillies and turmeric. Process to a paste. Heat the oil in a wok or pan, and fry the paste for 2 minutes. Remove the pan from the heat and add the fish.

3 Stir the coconut milk into the reserved stock and pour the mixture into a large saucepan. Add enough water to make up to 2.5 litres/ 4 pints/10 cups. In a jug (pitcher), mix the rice flour and gram flour to a thin cream with some stock. Stir into the mixture. Bring to the boil, stirring. Add the bamboo shoots to the saucepan and cook for about 10 minutes.

4 Stir in the fish mixture, season to taste with salt and ground black pepper, and cook until completely heated through. Guests take some noodles and pour the soup over them, then scatter over the egg wedges, onions, spring onions, prawns and chillies as a garnish.

Nutritional information per portion: Energy 344kcal/1436kJ; Protein 23.3g; Carbohydrate 18.5g, of which sugars 4g; Fat 18.3g, of which saturates 10.8g; Cholesterol 135mg; Calcium 87mg; Fibre 2.5g; Sodium 146mg.

Green fish curry

Any firm-fleshed fish can be used in this spicy dish, which gains its rich flavour from a mixture of fresh herbs, spices, lime and fresh chillies. A garnish of green chilli slices gives it extra heat.

SERVES 4

4 garlic cloves, coarsely chopped

5cm/2in piece fresh root ginger, peeled and
   coarsely chopped

2 fresh green chillies, seeded and
   coarsely chopped

grated rind and juice of 1 lime

5–10ml/1–2 tsp shrimp paste (optional)

5ml/1 tsp coriander seeds

5ml/1 tsp five-spice powder

75ml/6 tbsp sesame oil

2 red onions, finely chopped

900g/2lb hoki fillets, skinned

400ml/14fl oz/1²/₃ cups canned
   coconut milk

45ml/3 tbsp Thai fish sauce

50g/2oz/2 cups fresh coriander
   (cilantro) leaves

50g/2oz/2 cups fresh basil leaves

6 spring onions (scallions),
   coarsely chopped

150ml/¹/₄ pint/²/₃ cup sunflower or
   groundnut (peanut) oil

sliced fresh green chilli and finely chopped
   fresh coriander (cilantro),
   to garnish

cooked basmati or Thai fragrant rice
   and lime wedges, to serve

1 First make the curry paste. Combine the garlic, ginger, chillies, lime juice and shrimp paste, if using, in a food processor. Add the spices, with half the sesame oil. Process to a paste, then spoon into a bowl, cover and set aside.

2 Heat a wok or large, shallow pan, and pour in the remaining sesame oil. When it is hot, stir-fry the red onions over high heat for 2 minutes. Add the fish and stir-fry for 1–2 minutes to seal the fillets on all sides.

3 Lift out the red onions and fish with a slotted spoon and put them on a plate. Add the curry paste to the wok or pan and fry for 1 minute, stirring constantly. Return the fish and onions to the pan, pour in the coconut milk and bring to the boil. Lower the heat, add the Thai fish sauce and simmer gently for 5–7 minutes until the fish is cooked through and tender.

4 Process the herbs, spring onions, lime rind and sunflower or groundnut oil to a coarse paste. Stir into the fish curry. Garnish with chilli and coriander and serve with rice and lime wedges.

Nutritional information per portion: Energy 575kcal/2390kJ; Protein 40g; Carbohydrate 6.2g, of which sugars 4.9g; Fat 43.5g, of which saturates 5.9g; Cholesterol 6mg; Calcium 132mg; Fibre 0g; Sodium 362mg.

Monkfish with tomatoes and spices

This spicy fish stew makes a really delicious lunch or light supper dish. It would provide a more substantial meal if it was served with couscous and a tomato and onion salad.

SERVES 4

8 tomatoes
675g/1¹/₂lb monkfish
30ml/2 tbsp plain (all-purpose) flour
5ml/1 tsp ground coriander
2.5ml/¹/₂ tsp ground turmeric
25g/1oz/2 tbsp butter
2 garlic cloves, finely chopped

15–30ml/1–2 tbsp olive oil
40g/1¹/₂oz/4 tbsp pine nuts, toasted
1 preserved lemon, cut into pieces
12 black olives, pitted
salt and ground black pepper
whole slices of preserved lemon and chopped
    fresh parsley, to garnish

1 Peel the tomatoes by placing them briefly in boiling water, then cold water. Quarter the tomatoes, remove the cores and seeds and discard. Chop the tomato flesh roughly.

2 Cut the fish into bitesize chunks. Blend together the flour, coriander and turmeric, and season with salt and pepper to taste. Dust the fish with the seasoned flour and set aside.

3 Melt the butter in a non-stick frying pan and fry the tomatoes and garlic over low heat for 6–8 minutes, until the tomato mixture is very thick and most of the liquid has evaporated.

4 Push the tomatoes to the edge of the frying pan, moisten the pan with a little olive oil and fry the monkfish pieces in a single layer over medium heat for 3–5 minutes, turning frequently. You may have to do this in batches, so as the first batch cooks, place them on top of the tomatoes and fry the remaining fish, adding a little more oil to the pan, if necessary. When all the fish is cooked, add the pine nuts and stir, scraping the bottom of the pan to remove the glazed tomatoes. The sauce should be thick and slightly charred in places.

5 Rinse the preserved lemon in water, discard the pulp and cut the peel into strips. Add to the sauce with the olives, adjust the seasoning and serve garnished with slices of preserved lemon and parsley.

Nutritional information per portion: Energy 306kcal/1283kJ; Protein 29g; Carbohydrate 5.1g, of which sugars 5.1g; Fat 19.1g, of which saturates 5g; Cholesterol 38mg; Calcium 29mg; Fibre 1.8g; Sodium 203mg.

Halibut with peppers and coconut milk

This aromatic dish, known as moqueca, *comes from Brazil. Cooked and served in an earthenware dish, it is usually accompanied by rice and flavoured cassava flour to soak up the sauce.*

SERVES 6

16 halibut, cod, haddock or monkfish
    fillets, each about 115g/4oz
juice of 2 limes
8 fresh coriander (cilantro) sprigs
2 fresh red chillies, seeded and chopped
3 tomatoes, sliced into thin rounds
1 red (bell) pepper, seeded and sliced into
    thin rounds
1 green (bell) pepper, seeded and sliced
    into thin rounds
1 small onion, sliced into thin rounds
200ml/7fl oz/scant 1 cup coconut milk
60ml/4 tbsp palm oil
salt
cooked white rice, to serve

FOR THE CASSAVA FLOUR

30ml/2 tbsp palm oil
1 medium onion, thinly sliced
250g/9oz/2¼ cups cassava flour

1 Place the fish fillets in a large, shallow dish and pour over water to cover. Pour in the lime juice and set aside for 30 minutes. Drain the fish thoroughly and pat dry with kitchen paper. Arrange the fish in a single layer in a heavy pan which has a tight-fitting lid.

2 Sprinkle the coriander and chillies over the fish, then top with a layer each of tomatoes, peppers and onion. Pour the coconut milk over, cover and leave to stand for 15 minutes before cooking.

3 Season with salt, then place the pan over a high heat and cook until the coconut milk comes to the boil. Lower the heat and simmer for 5 minutes. Remove the lid, pour in the palm oil, cover again and simmer for 10 minutes.

4 Meanwhile make the flavoured cassava flour. Heat the oil in a large frying pan over a very low heat. Stir in the onion slices and cook for 8–10 minutes until soft and golden. Stir in the cassava flour and cook, stirring constantly, for 1–2 minutes until lightly toasted and evenly coloured by the oil. Season with salt. Serve the *moqueca* with the rice and flavoured cassava flour.

Nutritional information per portion: Energy 392Kcal/1648kJ; Protein 29g; Carbohydrate 50g, of which sugars 18g; Fat 8g, of which saturates 3g; Cholesterol 40mg; Calcium 80mg; Fibre 2g; Sodium 123mg.

Fish moolie

This is a popular South-east Asian fish curry in a coconut sauce. Choose a firm-textured fish so that the pieces stay intact during cooking. Monkfish, halibut or cod work well in this dish.

SERVES 4

500g/1¼lb monkfish or other firm-
    textured fish fillets, skinned and cut
    into 2.5cm/1in cubes
2.5ml/½ tsp salt
50g/2oz/⅔ cup desiccated (dry
    unsweetened shredded) coconut
6 shallots, chopped
6 blanched almonds
2–3 garlic cloves, roughly chopped
2.5cm/1in piece fresh root ginger, peeled
    and sliced
2 lemon grass stalks, trimmed
10ml/2 tsp ground turmeric
45ml/3 tbsp vegetable oil
2 x 400ml/14fl oz cans coconut milk
1–3 fresh red chillies, seeded and sliced
    into rings
salt and ground black pepper
fresh chives, to garnish
plain boiled basmati rice, to serve

1 Put the fish cubes in a shallow dish and sprinkle with the salt. Dry fry the coconut in a wok, turning all the time until it is crisp and golden, then transfer into a food processor and process to an oily paste. Scrape into a bowl and reserve.

2 Add the shallots, almonds, garlic and ginger to the food processor. Chop the bulbous part of each lemon grass stalk and add to the processor with the turmeric. Process the mixture to a paste. Bruise the remaining lemon grass stalks.

3 Heat the oil in a wok. Cook the shallot and spice mixture for about 2–3 minutes. Stir in the coconut milk and bring to the boil, stirring. Add the fish, most of the chilli and the lemon grass stalks. Cook for 3–4 minutes. Stir in the coconut paste and cook for a further 2–3 minutes. Season to taste.

4 Remove the lemon grass. Transfer the moolie to a dish and sprinkle with the remaining chilli. Garnish with chopped and whole chives and serve with rice.

Nutritional information per portion: Energy 319kcal/1335kJ; Protein 22.4g; Carbohydrate 16.7g, of which sugars 14.9g; Fat 18.6g, of which saturates 8.3g; Cholesterol 18mg; Calcium 96mg; Fibre 3g; Sodium 249mg.

Seafood in tamarind-laced coconut milk

Freshly ground spices produce a wonderful fragrant aroma in this curry, while the addition of tamarind paste gives a slightly sour note to the spicy coconut sauce.

SERVES 4

7.5ml/1½ tsp ground turmeric
5ml/1 tsp salt
450g/1lb monkfish fillet, cut into
　eight pieces
15ml/1 tbsp lemon juice
5ml/1 tsp cumin seeds
5ml/1 tsp coriander seeds
5ml/1 tsp black peppercorns
1 garlic clove, chopped
5cm/2in piece fresh root ginger,
　finely chopped

25g/1oz tamarind paste
150ml/¼ pint/⅔ cup hot water
30ml/2 tbsp vegetable oil
2 onions, halved and sliced lengthways
400ml/14fl oz/1⅔ cups coconut milk
4 mild green chillies, seeded and cut into
　thin strips
16 large prawns (shrimp), peeled
30ml/2 tbsp chopped fresh coriander
　(cilantro) leaves, to garnish

1 Mix together the ground turmeric and salt in a bowl. Place the fish in a shallow dish and sprinkle over the lemon juice, then rub the turmeric mixture over the fish. Cover and chill.

2 Put the cumin and coriander seeds and peppercorns in a blender or food processor and blend to a powder. Add the garlic and ginger and process for a few seconds more.

3 Preheat the oven to 200°C/400°F/Gas 6. Mix the tamarind paste and hot water and set aside. Heat the oil in a frying pan, add the onions and cook for 5–6 minutes, until softened and golden. Transfer the onions to a shallow ovenproof dish. Add the fish to the pan, and fry over a high heat, turning to seal on all sides. Remove from the pan and place on top of the onions.

4 Fry the ground spice mixture in the pan, stirring constantly, for 1–2 minutes. Stir in the tamarind liquid, coconut milk and chilli strips then bring to the boil. Pour over the fish. Cover the dish and cook in the oven for 10 minutes. Add the prawns, and cook for a further 5 minutes, or until the prawns are pink. Do not overcook or they will toughen. Check the seasoning, sprinkle with whole coriander leaves and serve.

Nutritional information per portion: Energy 220kcal/926kJ; Protein 28g; Carbohydrate 12.8g, of which sugars 10.5g; Fat 6.8g, of which saturates 1g; Cholesterol 113mg; Calcium 103mg; Fibre 1.4g; Sodium 720mg.

Spiced halibut and tomato curry

The chunky cubes of white fish contrast beautifully with the rich red spicy tomato sauce and absorb all the spicy flavours. You can use any type of firm white fish for this recipe.

SERVES 4

60ml/4 tbsp lemon juice
60ml/4 tbsp rice wine vinegar
30ml/2 tbsp cumin seeds
5ml/1 tsp turmeric
5ml/1 tsp chilli powder
5ml/1 tsp salt
750g/1lb 11oz thick halibut fillets,
    skinned and cubed
60ml/4 tbsp sunflower oil
1 onion, finely chopped
3 garlic cloves, finely chopped
30ml/2 tbsp grated fresh root ginger
10ml/2 tsp black mustard seeds
2 x 400g/14oz cans chopped tomatoes
5ml/1 tsp sugar
chopped coriander (cilantro) leaves and
    sliced green chilli, to garnish
basmati rice, pickles and poppadums,
    to serve
natural (plain) yogurt, to drizzle

1 Mix together the lemon juice, vinegar, cumin, turmeric, chilli powder and salt in a shallow non-metallic bowl. Add the cubed fish and turn to coat evenly. Cover and put in the refrigerator to marinate for 25–30 minutes.

2 Meanwhile, heat a wok or large frying pan over high heat and add the oil. When hot, carefully add the onion, garlic, ginger and mustard seeds. Reduce the heat to low and cook very gently for about 10 minutes, stirring occasionally. Add the tomatoes and sugar to the pan and bring to the boil.

3 Reduce the heat, cover the pan and cook gently for about 15–20 minutes, stirring occasionally.

4 Add the fish and its marinade to the pan, stir gently to mix, then cover and simmer gently for 15–20 minutes, or until the fish is cooked through and the flesh flakes easily with a fork.

5 Serve the curry ladled into shallow bowls with basmati rice, pickles and poppadums. Garnish with fresh coriander and green chillies, and drizzle over some natural yogurt.

Nutritional information per portion: Energy 335kcal/1409kJ; Protein 41.9g; Carbohydrate 8.4g, of which sugars 8.1g; Fat 15.2g, of which saturates 2.1g; Cholesterol 66mg; Calcium 73mg; Fibre 2.2g; Sodium 622mg.

Jamaican fish curry

This recipe uses some of the warm spices that are common to Caribbean cuisine. The taste in that region is for strong, pungent flavours rather than fiery heat.

SERVES 4

2 halibut steaks, total weight about
   500–675g/1¼–1½lb
30ml/2 tbsp groundnut (peanut) oil
2 cardamom pods
1 cinnamon stick
6 allspice berries
4 cloves
1 large onion, chopped
3 garlic cloves, crushed
10–15ml/2–3 tsp grated fresh root ginger
10ml/2 tsp ground cumin
5ml/1 tsp ground coriander
2.5ml/½ tsp cayenne pepper
4 tomatoes, peeled, seeded and chopped
1 sweet potato, about 225g/8oz, cubed
475ml/16fl oz/2 cups fish stock or water
120ml/4fl oz/½ cup coconut cream
1 bay leaf
225g/8oz/generous 1 cup white long
   grain rice
salt

1 Rub the halibut steaks well with salt and set aside.

2 Heat the oil in a heavy pan and stir-fry the cardamom pods, cinnamon stick, allspice berries and cloves for about 3 minutes.

3 Add the onion, garlic and ginger. Continue cooking for about 4–5 minutes over low heat until the onion is soft. Add the cumin, coriander and cayenne pepper and cook briefly, stirring all the time. Stir in the tomatoes, sweet potato, fish stock or water, coconut and bay leaf.

4 Season with salt and bring to the boil, then lower the heat, cover and cook for 15 minutes.

5 Cook the rice according to your preferred method. Meanwhile, add the halibut steaks to the pan of sauce and spoon the sauce over to cover them. Cover the pan and simmer gently for 10 minutes until the fish is tender and flakes easily.

6 Spoon the rice into a warmed serving dish, spoon over the curry sauce and arrange the halibut steaks on top and serve.

Nutritional information per portion: Energy 639kcal/2669kJ; Protein 34.2g; Carbohydrate 62g, of which sugars 8.3g; Fat 28.4g, of which saturates 18.7g; Cholesterol 44mg; Calcium 74mg; Fibre 2.4g; Sodium 115mg.

Sour fish, star fruit and chilli stew

This refreshing dish is just one of many variations on the theme of sour fish stew found in South-east Asia. The star fruit are added toward the end of cooking so that they retain a bite.

SERVES 4–6

30ml/2 tbsp coconut or palm oil
900ml/1½ pints/3¾ cups water
2 lemon grass stalks, bruised
25g/1oz fresh root ginger, finely sliced
about 675g/1½lb trout, cut into steaks
2 firm star fruit (carambola), thinly sliced
juice of 1–2 limes

FOR THE SPICE PASTE

4 shallots, chopped
4 fresh red chillies, seeded and chopped
2 garlic cloves, chopped
25g/1oz galangal, chopped
25g/1oz fresh turmeric, chopped
3–4 macadamia nuts, chopped
1 bunch fresh basil , 1 lime, cut into
    wedges and plain basmati rice, to serve

1 Using a mortar and pestle or food processor, grind all the spice paste ingredients together to form a coarse paste.

2 Heat the oil in a wok or wide, heavy pan, stir in the spice paste and fry until fragrant. Add the water, lemon grass and ginger. Bring to the boil, stirring, then reduce the heat and simmer for 10 minutes. Slip the fish steaks into the pan, making sure there is enough liquid to cover the fish. Add more water if necessary.

3 Simmer the mixture gently for 3–4 minutes, then add the star fruit and lime juice to the pan. Simmer for about 2–3 minutes more, until the fish is cooked through.

4 Divide the fish and star fruit among four to six warmed serving bowls and add a little of the cooking liquid to each. Garnish with basil leaves and a wedge of lime. Serve the stew with bowls of steamed rice, moistened by the remaining cooking liquid.

Nutritional information per portion: Energy 240kcal/1001kJ; Protein 25.9g; Carbohydrate 7.3g, of which sugars 4.7g; Fat 12.1g, of which saturates 1.2g; Cholesterol 0mg; Calcium 27mg; Fibre 1.7g; Sodium 67mg.

Fish curry in a rich tomato sauce

A tomato-based sauce is used to add colour and flavour in this tasty fish dish. The spicing is light so that the delicate fish is not overwhelmed.

SERVES 4

675g/1¹/₂lb steaks of firm-textured fish
    such as tuna or monkfish, skinned
30ml/2 tbsp lemon juice
5ml/1 tsp salt
5ml/1 tsp ground turmeric
vegetable oil, for shallow-frying
40g/1¹/₂oz/¹/₂ cup plain (all-purpose) flour
1.5ml/¹/₄ tsp ground black pepper
60ml/4 tbsp vegetable oil
10ml/2 tsp sugar
1 large onion, finely chopped
15ml/1 tbsp grated fresh root ginger
15ml/1 tbsp crushed garlic
5ml/1 tsp ground coriander
2.5–5ml/¹/₂–1 tsp hot chilli powder
175g/6oz can chopped tomatoes,
    300ml/¹/₂ pint/1¹/₄ cups warm water
30ml/2 tbsp chopped fresh coriander
    (cilantro) leaves, to garnish
plain boiled rice, to serve

1 Cut the fish into 7.5cm/3in pieces and put into a bowl. Add the lemon juice and sprinkle with half the salt and half the turmeric. Mix gently and set aside for 15 minutes.

2 Pour some oil into a 23cm/9in frying pan to a depth of 1cm/¹/₂in and heat to medium. Mix the flour and pepper and dust the fish in the seasoned flour. Fry until browned on both sides. Drain on kitchen paper.

3 In a large pan, heat 60ml/4 tbsp oil. When the oil is hot, but not smoking, add the sugar and let it caramelize.

4 When the sugar is brown, add the onion, ginger and garlic and fry for 7–8 minutes, until beginning to colour. Stir regularly. Add the ground coriander, chilli powder and the remaining turmeric. Stir-fry for 30 seconds and add the tomatoes. Cook until soft and the oil separates from the paste.

5 Add the warm water and the remaining salt to the pan, and bring to the boil. Add the fish, reduce the heat to low and simmer, uncovered, for 5–6 minutes. Garnish with the coriander leaves and serve with plain boiled rice.

Nutritional information per portion: Energy 242kcal/1010kJ; Protein 22.2g; Carbohydrate 6.4g, of which sugars 5.5g; Fat 14.3g, of which saturates 1.9g; Cholesterol 43mg; Calcium 65mg; Fibre 1.6g; Sodium 182mg.

Fish curry with chillies, shallots and lemon grass

This is a thin, soupy curry with the characteristically aromatic Thai flavourings of lemon grass, garlic, chillies, and the classic fish sauce to add a hint of piquancy.

SERVES 4

450g/1lb salmon fillet
500ml/17fl oz/2¼ cups vegetable stock
4 shallots, finely chopped
2 garlic cloves, finely chopped
2.5cm/1in piece fresh galangal,
finely chopped
1 lemon grass stalk, finely chopped
2.5ml/½ tsp dried chilli flakes
15ml/1 tbsp Thai fish sauce
5ml/1 tsp palm sugar (jaggery) or light
muscovado (brown) sugar

1 Place the salmon fillet in the freezer for 30–40 minutes to firm up the flesh for slicing.

2 Remove and discard the skin on the salmon, then use a sharp knife to cut the fish into bitesize pieces, about 2.5cm/1in cubes, removing any stray bones with your fingers or with tweezers as you do so.

3 Pour the vegetable stock into a large, heavy pan and bring it to the boil over medium heat.

4 Add the shallots, garlic, galangal, lemon grass, chilli flakes, fish sauce and sugar. Bring back to the boil, stir well, then reduce the heat and simmer gently for 15 minutes.

5 Add the fish to the pan, bring the mixture back to the boil, then turn off the heat.

6 Leave the curry to stand for 10–15 minutes until the fish is cooked through, then serve in warmed bowls.

Nutritional information per portion: Energy 212kcal/882kJ; Protein 23.1g; Carbohydrate 1.7g, of which sugars 1.6g; Fat 12.5g, of which saturates 2.2g; Cholesterol 56mg; Calcium 28mg; Fibre 0.2g; Sodium 267mg.

Sour fish curry

In this curry, the spice paste is fried before it is added to the sauce. A little coconut milk is also added to temper the tartness of the tamarind, giving the dish a much richer flavour.

SERVES 4

500g/1¼lb thick fish cutlets
1 aubergine (eggplant)
2 tomatoes
30ml/2 tbsp tamarind concentrate
350ml/12 floz/1½ cups water
45ml/3 tbsp coconut milk
5ml/1 tsp sugar
30ml/2 tbsp vegetable oil
15ml/1 tbsp chilli oil (optional)
salt

FOR THE SPICE PASTE

2 dried red chillies, softened in
    warm water, seeded and chopped
½ large onion, chopped
15g/½oz fresh turmeric
15g/½oz shrimp paste
3 garlic cloves, chopped

1 Cut the fish into large pieces and rub with about 5ml/1 tsp salt. Slice the aubergine lengthways then slice crossways. Quarter the tomatoes.

2 To make the spice paste, grind all the ingredients together using a mortar and pestle or a food processor. Heat the oil and fry the paste until it is fragrant.

3 Blend the tamarind concentrate with the water and stir it into the fried spice paste. Add the coconut milk, fish, aubergine and tomato. Simmer for 8 minutes until the fish is cooked.

4 Season with salt and sugar. If you wish, add a swirl of chilli oil to give the dish a rich colour.

Nutritional information per portion: Energy 205Kcal/860kJ; Protein 26.5g; Carbohydrate 9.4g, of which sugars 8.9g; Fat 7.1g, of which saturates 1g; Cholesterol 76mg; Calcium 79mg; Fibre 2.7g; Sodium 257mg.

Curried coconut salmon

Salmon is a robustly flavoured fish, which is delicious cooked with a blend of spices, garlic and chilli, as in this curry. It is cooked in a slow cooker, allowing all the tastes to develop well.

SERVES 4

15ml/1 tbsp vegetable oil
1 onion, finely chopped
2 fresh green chillies, seeded and chopped
2 garlic cloves, crushed
2.5cm/1in piece fresh root ginger, grated
175ml/6fl oz/³⁄₄ cup coconut milk
10ml/2 tsp ground cumin
5ml/1 tsp ground coriander

4 salmon steaks, each about 175g/6oz
10ml/2 tsp chilli powder
2.5ml/¹⁄₂ tsp ground turmeric
15ml/1 tbsp white or red wine vinegar
1.5ml/¹⁄₄ tsp salt
fresh coriander (cilantro) sprigs, to garnish
rice tossed with spring onions (scallions), to
    serve

1 Heat the oil in a pan, add the onion, chillies, garlic and ginger and fry for about 5–6 minutes, until fairly soft. Place in a food processor or blender with 120ml/4fl oz/¹⁄₂ cup of the coconut milk and blend until smooth.

2 Transfer the paste into the ceramic cooking pot. Stir in 5ml/1 tsp of the cumin, the ground coriander and the rest of the coconut milk. Cover and cook on high for 1¹⁄₂ hours.

3 About 20 minutes before the end of cooking time, arrange the salmon steaks in a single layer in a shallow glass dish. Combine the remaining 5ml/1 tsp cumin, the chilli powder, turmeric, vinegar and salt in a bowl to make a paste. Rub the mixture over the salmon steaks and leave to marinate at room temperature while the sauce finishes cooking.

4 Add the salmon steaks to the sauce, arranging them in a single layer, and spoon some of the coconut sauce over the top to keep the fish moist while it cooks. Cover with the lid, reduce the temperature to low and cook for 45 minutes–1 hour, or until the salmon is opaque and tender.

5 Transfer the fish to a serving dish, spoon over the sauce and garnish with fresh coriander sprigs. Serve immediately with the rice.

Nutritional information per portion: Energy 363kcal/1512kJ; Protein 35.9g; Carbohydrate 5.1g, of which sugars 4.2g; Fat 22.2g, of which saturates 3.8g; Cholesterol 88mg; Calcium 59mg; Fibre 0.5g; Sodium 275mg.

Malay fish curry

The fish curries of Malaysia differ slightly from region to region, but most of them include Indian spices and coconut milk. The Malay food stalls often feature a fish, chicken or beef curry, which is usually served with bread or rice, pickles and extra chillies.

SERVES 4

30ml/2 tbsp vegetable oil
7.5ml/1¹/₂ tsp tamarind paste
8 thick fish cutlets, about 90g/3¹/₂oz, such
   as grouper, red snapper, trout or mackerel
800ml/1¹/₂ pints coconut milk
salt
fresh coriander (cilantro) leaves, roughly
   chopped, to garnish
rice or crusty bread, to serve

FOR THE CURRY PASTE
4 shallots, chopped
4 garlic cloves, chopped
50g/2oz fresh root ginger, peeled
   and chopped
25g/1oz fresh turmeric, chopped
4–6 dried red chillies, softened in warm
   water, seeded and chopped
15ml/1 tbsp coriander seeds, roasted
15ml/1 tbsp cumin seeds, roasted
10ml/2 tsp fish curry powder
5ml/1 tsp fennel seeds
2.5ml/¹/₂ tsp black peppercorns

1 First make the curry paste. Using a mortar and pestle or food processor, grind the shallots, garlic, ginger, turmeric and chillies to a paste and transfer to a bowl.

2 Again, using the mortar and pestle or food processor, grind the roasted coriander and cumin seeds, fish curry powder, fennel seeds and peppercorns to a powder and add to the paste in the bowl. Bind with 15ml/1 tbsp water and thoroughly mix together.

3 Heat the oil in a wok or heavy pan. Stir in the curry paste and fry until fragrant. Add the tamarind paste and mix well. Add the fish cutlets and cook for 1 minute on each side. Pour in the coconut milk, mix well and bring to the boil.

4 Reduce the heat and simmer for 10–15 minutes until the fish is cooked. Season to taste with salt. Scatter the coriander over the top and serve with plain or yellow rice, or with chunks of crusty bread to mop up the sauce.

Nutritional information per portion: Energy 264Kcal/1109kJ; Protein 36.6g; Carbohydrate 12.7g, of which sugars 12.1g; Fat 7.7g, of which saturates 1.3g; Cholesterol 89mg; Calcium 110mg; Fibre 1g; Sodium 354mg.

Indian shellfish and potato curry

This delicious dish is made with a freshly prepared spice paste, and roasted fennel and mustard seeds are stirred in at the end of cooking to impart all their fresh fragrance. In India this curry would generally be eaten with a yogurt dish, chutney, and flatbread to scoop it up, but it could also be served with rice.

SERVES 4

30ml/2 tbsp ghee, or 15ml/1 tbsp vegetable
   oil and 15g/¹/₂oz/1 tbsp butter
1 onion, halved lengthways and sliced along
   the grain
a handful of curry leaves
1 cinnamon stick
2–3 medium-size waxy potatoes, lightly
   steamed, peeled and diced
500g/1¹/₄lb fresh large prawns (shrimp),
   peeled and deveined
200ml/7fl oz/scant 1 cup coconut milk
10ml/2 tsp fennel seeds

10ml/2 tsp brown mustard seeds
salt and ground black pepper
fresh coriander (cilantro) leaves, roughly
   chopped, to garnish

FOR THE SPICE PASTE

4 garlic cloves, chopped
25g/1oz fresh root ginger, peeled
   and chopped
2 red chillies, seeded and chopped
5ml/1 tsp ground turmeric
15ml/1 tbsp fish curry powder

1 To make the spice paste, grind the garlic, ginger and chillies to a coarse paste using a mortar and pestle or a food processor. Stir in the turmeric and curry powder.

2 Heat the ghee in a heavy pan or earthenware pot. Stir in the onion and fry until golden. Stir in the curry leaves, followed by the cinnamon stick and the spice paste. Fry until fragrant, then add the potatoes, coating them in the spices.

3 Toss the prawns into the pan and cook for 12 minutes. Stir in the coconut milk and bubble it up to thicken and reduce it. Season with salt and pepper to taste.

4 Roast the fennel and mustard seeds in a small heavy pan until they begin to pop and give off a nutty aroma. Stir them into the curry and serve immediately, sprinkled with a little chopped coriander.

Nutritional information per portion: Energy 204kcal/857kJ; Protein 23.5g; Carbohydrate 13.5g, of which sugars 5.2g; Fat 6.6g, of which saturates 0.9g; Cholesterol 244mg; Calcium 126mg; Fibre 1g; Sodium 299mg.

Curried prawns in coconut milk

This is a mildly spiced dish in which the prawns are cooked in a tangy coconut gravy along with cherry tomatoes. It is simple but flavoursome and very quick to prepare.

SERVES 4–6

600ml/1 pint/2$\frac{1}{2}$ cups coconut milk
30ml/2 tbsp yellow curry paste
2.5ml/$\frac{1}{2}$ tsp salt
5ml/1 tsp sugar
450g/1lb king prawns (jumbo shrimp),
    peeled, tails left intact, deveined
225g/8oz cherry tomatoes
fresh red chilli strips and coriander
    (cilantro) leaves, to garnish
juice of $\frac{1}{2}$ lime, to serve

1 Pour half the coconut milk into a large heavy pan or wok and bring the mixture slowly to the boil.

2 Add the curry paste to the coconut milk in the pan, stir until it disperses, then simmer gently for about 10 minutes.

3 Add the salt, sugar and the remaining coconut milk to the pan. Simmer for another 5 minutes.

4 Add the prawns and cherry tomatoes to the pan. Simmer very gently over a low heat for about 5 minutes until the prawns are pink and tender.

5 Serve the prawns garnished with chilli strips and fresh coriander and have the lime juice on hand for sprinkling over.

Nutritional information per portion: Energy 118kcal/500kJ; Protein 14.1g; Carbohydrate 11g, of which sugars 11g; Fat 2.3g, of which saturates 0.6g; Cholesterol 146mg; Calcium 116mg; Fibre 0.4g; Sodium 466mg.

Goan prawn curry

Goan dishes use generous amounts of chilli, mellowed by coconut milk and palm vinegar. In this delicious coconut-enriched prawn curry, cider vinegar is a good alternative to palm vinegar.

SERVES 4

500g/1¼lb peeled king or tiger prawns
(jumbo shrimp)
2.5ml/½ tsp salt, plus extra to taste
30ml/2 tbsp palm vinegar
60ml/4 tbsp sunflower or olive oil
1 large onion, finely chopped
10ml/2 tsp crushed fresh root ginger
10ml/2 tsp crushed garlic
2.5ml/½ tsp ground cumin
5ml/1 tsp ground coriander
2.5ml/½ tsp ground turmeric
2.5ml/½ tsp chilli powder
2.5ml/½ tsp ground black pepper
75g/3oz/1 cup creamed coconut,
chopped, or 250ml/8floz/1 cup
coconut cream
4 green chillies
30ml/2 tbsp chopped fresh coriander
(cilantro) leaves
plain boiled rice, to serve

1 Put the prawns in a bowl and add the measured salt and vinegar. Mix and set aside for 10–15 minutes.

2 Heat the sunflower or olive oil in a medium pan and add the onion. Fry over medium heat until the onion is translucent. Add the ginger and garlic and fry for about 2 minutes over a low heat, until lightly browned.

3 Mix the cumin, coriander, turmeric, chilli powder and pepper in a bowl and add 30ml/2 tbsp water to make a pouring consistency. Add to the onion and cook, stirring, for 4–5 minutes until the mixture is dry and the oil separates from the spice mix. Add 200ml/7fl oz/¾ cup warm water, the creamed coconut and salt to taste. Stir until the coconut has dissolved.

4 Add the prawns with the juices in the bowl, bring the pan to the boil, reduce the heat and cook for 5–7 minutes. Add the whole chillies and simmer for 2–3 minutes. Stir in the chopped coriander. Serve with plain rice.

Nutritional information per portion: Energy 171kcal/723kJ; Protein 21.9g; Carbohydrate 10g, of which sugars 7.4g; Fat 5.3g, of which saturates 2.5g; Cholesterol 227mg; Calcium 136mg; Fibre 1g; Sodium 344mg.

Prawn and cauliflower curry

This is a basic fisherman's curry that is simple to make, but incredibly tasty. In Thailand, this type of curry would usually be eaten from a communal bowl.

SERVES 4

450g/1lb raw tiger prawns (jumbo shrimp), peeled, deveined and cleaned

juice of 1 lime

15ml/1 tbsp vegetable oil

1 red onion, roughly chopped

2 garlic cloves, roughly chopped

2 Thai chillies, seeded and finely chopped

1 cauliflower, broken into florets

5ml/1 tsp sugar

2 star anise, dry-fried and ground

10ml/2 tsp fenugreek, dry-fried and ground

450ml/³⁄₄ pint/2 cups coconut milk

1 bunch fresh coriander (cilantro), chopped, to garnish

salt and ground black pepper

1 In a bowl, toss the prawns in the lime juice and set aside. Heat a wok or heavy pan and add the oil. Stir in the onion, garlic and chillies. As they brown, add the cauliflower to the pan. Stir-fry for 2–3 minutes.

2 Stir the sugar and spices into the pan. Add the coconut milk, stirring to make sure it is thoroughly combined. Reduce the heat and simmer for 10–15 minutes, or until the liquid has reduced and thickened a little.

3 Add the prawns and lime juice and cook for 1–2 minutes, or until the prawns turn pink. Season to taste, and sprinkle with coriander. Serve immediately.

COOK'S TIP

To devein prawns, make a shallow cut down the back of the prawn, lift out the thin, black vein and discard, then rinse the prawns thoroughly under cold running water.

Nutritional information per portion: Energy 157kcal/664kJ; Protein 24.7g; Carbohydrate 10.4g, of which sugars 9.4g; Fat 2.2g, of which saturates 0.6g; Cholesterol 219mg; Calcium 169mg; Fibre 2.7g; Sodium 351mg.

Yellow prawn curry

This South-east Asian speciality lives up to its name with an intense yellow colour, derived from the addition of turmeric, which adds a robust flavour.

SERVES 4

30ml/2 tbsp coconut or palm oil
2 shallots, finely chopped
2 garlic cloves, finely chopped
2 red chillies, seeded and finely chopped
25g/1oz fresh turmeric, finely chopped,
    or 10ml/2 tsp ground turmeric
25g/1oz fresh root ginger, finely chopped
2 lemon grass stalks, finely sliced
10ml/2 tsp coriander seeds
10ml/2 tsp shrimp paste
1 red (bell) pepper, seeded and sliced
4 kaffir lime leaves
about 500g/1¼lb fresh prawns (shrimp),
    shelled and deveined
400g/14oz can coconut milk
salt and ground black pepper
1 green chilli, seeded and sliced, to
    garnish
cooked rice and 4 fresh chillies, seeded
    and sliced, to serve

1 Heat the oil in a frying pan. Stir in the shallots, garlic, chillies, turmeric, ginger, lemon grass and coriander seeds and fry for a few minutes. Stir in the shrimp paste and cook for 2–3 minutes.

2 Add the red pepper and lime leaves and stir-fry for 1 minute. Add the prawns with the coconut milk. Stir to mix, and bring to the boil.

3 Cook the mixture for 5–6 minutes until the prawns become pink and are cooked. Season to taste with salt and pepper.

4 Spoon the prawns on to a warmed serving dish and sprinkle with the sliced green chilli to garnish. Serve the curry with rice and the sliced fresh chillies on the side.

Nutritional information per portion: Energy 230kcal/965kJ; Protein 26.4g; Carbohydrate 16g, of which sugars 13.5g; Fat 7.2g, of which saturates 1g; Cholesterol 263mg; Calcium 226mg; Fibre 2.7g; Sodium 519mg.

Prawn korma

This delectable prawn curry features almonds and yogurt, along with poppy and sesame seeds, which are a cooling addition, in contrast to the heat of the chilli, garlic and ginger.

SERVES 4

50g/2oz/¹/₂ cup blanched almonds

500g/1¹/₄ lb raw peeled king prawns (jumbo shrimp)

30ml/2 tbsp lemon juice

2.5ml/¹/₂ tsp ground turmeric

15ml/1 tbsp white poppy seeds

15ml/1 tbsp sesame seeds

150g/5oz/²/₃ cup natural (plain) yogurt

7.5ml/1¹/₂ tsp gram flour

60ml/4 tbsp sunflower or olive oil

1 large onion, finely chopped

10ml/2 tsp ginger purée (paste)

10ml/2 tsp garlic purée (paste)

1.5–2.5ml/¹/₄–¹/₂ tsp chilli powder

5ml/1 tsp salt, or to taste

15ml/1 tbsp toasted flaked (sliced) almonds, to garnish

1 Soak the almonds in 150ml/¹/₄ pint/²/₃ cup boiling water for 20 minutes. Meanwhile, in a large mixing bowl, mix the prawns, lemon juice and turmeric together. Set aside. Grind the poppy and sesame seeds in a coffee grinder or blender until they are finely ground, about the consistency of salt. Whisk the yogurt and gram flour together and set aside.

2 In a heavy pan, heat the oil and add the onion. Fry gently until the onion is soft and translucent, which will take around 5–6 minutes. Add the ginger and garlic, the ground poppy and sesame seeds, and the chilli powder. Cook for 2–3 minutes, stirring, then add the prawns, salt and the yogurt. Reduce the heat to low, cover the pan with a lid and cook for another 3–4 minutes.

3 Meanwhile, purée the almonds with the water in which they were soaked in a food processor or blender, and then add this to the prawns. Stir to mix well and cook for a further 5–6 minutes or until the prawns have curled up at the ends. Transfer the korma to a serving dish and garnish with the toasted almonds before serving.

Nutritional information per portion: Energy 143kcal/601kJ; Protein 20.4g; Carbohydrate 5.4g, of which sugars 2.7g; Fat 4.8g, of which saturates 0.7g; Cholesterol 195mg; Calcium 168mg; Fibre 0.6g; Sodium 230mg.

Crab in roasted coconut sauce

This is a hot curry, but you can adjust the level of pungency to taste by using fewer green chillies.
If you prefer, frozen crab claws may be used, or pre-prepared crabs, with all the juices.

SERVES 4

2 large fresh uncooked crabs, about
    400g/14oz each
75g/3oz/1 cup desiccated (dry
    unsweetened shredded) coconut
3 cloves
10 black peppercorns
5–6 dried red chillies
15ml/1 tbsp coriander seeds
5ml/1 tsp cumin seeds
45ml/3 tbsp sunflower oil or plain olive oil
1 large onion, finely chopped
5ml/1 tsp ginger purée
5ml/1 tsp garlic purée
1–2 green chillies, finely chopped
    (seeded if preferred)
2.5ml/½ tsp ground turmeric
3.5ml/¾ tsp salt, or to taste
25ml/1½ tbsp tamarind juice
plain boiled basmati rice, to serve

1 Place each crab on its back and twist to remove the claws and legs, and the feathery toes. Pull the centre portion from the main shell and remove the stomach sac, gills and lungs. Extract the meat, then wash the claws and legs.

2 In a small heavy pan, dry-roast the coconut over a low heat, stirring constantly until lightly browned. Remove the coconut and wipe the pan clean.

3 Dry-roast the cloves, peppercorns, dried chillies, coriander and cumin seeds for about 1 minute until they release their aroma. Remove and allow to cool. Grind the roasted coconut and the spices in a blender, and set aside. Heat the oil over a medium heat and fry the onion, ginger, garlic and green chillies for 8–10 minutes or until the mixture is just beginning to brown.

4 Add the turmeric, crab pieces, but not the meat, and salt. Pour in 350ml/12fl oz/1½ cups water and add the ground spices. Cook for 3–4 minutes, then add the crab meat. Cook for 2–3 minutes, then add the tamarind juice. Stir, cook for 1 minute, then serve with plain basmati rice.

Nutritional information per portion: Energy 295kcal/1223kJ; Protein 11.4g; Carbohydrate 11.7g, of which sugars 6.8g; Fat 23.1g, of which saturates 11.2g; Cholesterol 22mg; Calcium 55mg; Fibre 4g; Sodium 648mg.

Squid in hot yellow sauce

Simple fishermen's dishes such as this one are cooked the length and breadth of Malaysia's coastline. To temper the heat, the dish is often served with a classic salad of finely shredded green mango that has been tossed in lime juice.

SERVES 4

500g/1¼lb fresh squid
juice of 2 limes
5ml/1 tsp salt
4 shallots, chopped
4 garlic cloves, chopped
25g/1oz galangal, chopped
25g/1oz fresh turmeric, chopped
6–8 red chillies, seeded and
   finely chopped
30ml/2 tbsp vegetable or groundnut
   (peanut) oil
7.5ml/1½ tsp palm sugar (jaggery)
2 lemon grass stalks, crushed
4 lime leaves
400ml/14fl oz/1⅔ cups coconut milk
salt and ground black pepper
crusty bread or steamed rice, to serve

1 First prepare the squid. Hold the body sac in one hand and pull off the head with the other. Sever the tentacles just above the eyes, and discard the rest of the head and innards. Clean the body sac inside and out and remove the skin. Pat the squid dry, cut it into thick slices and put them in a bowl, along with the tentacles. Mix the lime juice with the salt and rub it into the squid. Set aside for 30 minutes.

2 Meanwhile, using a mortar and pestle, food processor or blender, grind the shallots, garlic, galangal, turmeric and chillies until they form a coarse paste.

3 Heat the oil in a wok or heavy pan, and stir in the coarse paste. Cook the paste until fragrant, then stir in the palm sugar, lemon grass and lime leaves. Drain the squid of any juice and toss it around the wok, coating it in the flavourings.

4 Pour the coconut milk into the pan and bring it to the boil. Reduce the heat to low and simmer for 5–10 minutes, until the squid is tender. Take care not to overcook the squid or it will become rubbery. Season to taste with salt and ground black pepper and serve the curry immediately with chunks of fresh, crusty bread or steamed rice.

Nutritional information per portion: Energy 185kcal/780kJ; Protein 19.8g; Carbohydrate 9.4g, of which sugars 7.6g; Fat 8g, of which saturates 1.4g; Cholesterol 281mg; Calcium 50mg; Fibre 0.2g; Sodium 739mg.

Fiery octopus

Here octopus is stir-fried to give it a rich meaty texture, then smothered in a fiery chilli sauce.
The dish combines the charred octopus flavour with traditional Korean spiciness and the zing
of chillies. Serve with steamed rice and a bowl of soup.

SERVES 2

2 small octopuses, cleaned and gutted
15ml/1 tbsp vegetable oil
1/2 onion, sliced 5mm/1/4 in thick
1/4 carrot, thinly sliced
1/2 leek, thinly sliced
75g/3oz jalapeño chillies, trimmed
2 garlic cloves, crushed
10ml/2 tsp Korean chilli powder
5ml/1 tsp dark soy sauce
45ml/3 tbsp gochujang chilli paste
30ml/2 tbsp mirin or rice wine
15ml/1 tbsp maple syrup
sesame oil and sesame seeds, to garnish

1 First blanch the octopuses in boiling water to soften slightly. Drain well, and cut into pieces approximately 5cm/2in long.

2 Heat the oil in a frying pan over a medium-high heat and add the onion, carrot, leek and chillies. Stir-fry for 3 minutes. Add the octopus and garlic, and add the chilli powder.

3 Stir-fry for 3–4 minutes, or until the octopus is tender. Add the soy sauce, gochujang chilli paste, mirin or rice wine, and the maple syrup. Mix well and stir-fry for another minute more.

4 Transfer to a serving platter, and garnish with a drizzle of sesame oil and a sprinkling of sesame seeds.

Nutritional information per portion: Energy 235kcal/988kJ; Protein 28.6g; Carbohydrate 13.2g, of which sugars 11.9g; Fat 8g, of which saturates 1.2g; Cholesterol 72mg; Calcium 76mg; Fibre 2.4g; Sodium 204mg.

Poultry Curries

Chicken, guinea fowl and duck all lend themselves to robust seasonings, from zesty Asian flavours to fiery chillies and warm spices. Poultry is a great partner for rich, aromatic herbs and spices that complement without overpowering. In this section, poultry is given various tasty treatments – from Creamy Chicken Korma to Gochujang Chicken Curry, and Tandoori Chicken to Chinese Duck Curry.

Tandoori Chicken

Tandoori refers to a method of cooking in a charcoal-fired clay oven, a tandoor. In northern India and Pakistan, many foods are cooked in this way, but in western countries it is popular for chicken.

SERVES 4

30ml/2 tbsp vegetable oil
2 small onions, cut into wedges
2 garlic cloves, sliced
4 skinless chicken breast fillets,
    cut into cubes
100ml/3¹/₂fl oz/¹/₃ cup water
300g/11oz jar tandoori sauce
salt and ground black pepper
fresh coriander (cilantro) sprigs,
    to garnish

TO SERVE

5ml/1 tsp ground turmeric
350g/12oz/1²/₃ cups basmati rice

1 Heat the oil in a flameproof casserole. Add the onions and garlic, and cook for about 3 minutes, or until the onion is beginning to soften, stirring frequently.

2 Add the cubes of chicken to the casserole and cook for 6 minutes. Stir the water into the tandoori sauce and pour it over the chicken. Bring to the boil, then reduce the heat and simmer for 10 minutes, or until the chicken pieces are cooked through and the sauce is slightly reduced and thickened.

3 Meanwhile, bring a large pan of lightly salted water to the boil, add the turmeric and rice and bring back to the boil. Stir once, reduce the heat to prevent the water from boiling over and simmer the rice for 12 minutes, or according to the time suggested on the packet, until tender.

4 Drain the rice well and serve immediately alongside the tandoori chicken on warmed individual serving plates, garnished with the sprigs of fresh coriander.

Nutritional information per portion: Energy 592kcal/2479kJ; Protein 44g; Carbohydrate 77.5g, of which sugars 4.5g; Fat 11.4g, of which saturates 1.1g; Cholesterol 105mg; Calcium 54mg; Fibre 0.4g; Sodium 826mg.

Chicken Murgh

This butter chicken is rich and creamy, so it is not surprising it is one of the most popular Indian dishes. The addition of several spices to the chicken and the sauce ensures that it is very tasty.

SERVES 4

FOR THE CHICKEN TIKKA
juice of 1/2 lemon
5ml/1 tsp salt or to taste
675g/1 1/2 lb skinless chicken breast
    fillets, cut into 5cm/2in cubes
120ml/4floz/1/2 cup Greek (US strained
    plain) yogurt
15ml/1 tbsp crushed garlic
15ml/1 tbsp crushed fresh ginger
2.5ml/1/2 tsp ground turmeric
5ml/1 tsp garam masala
2.5ml/1/2 tsp chilli powder
10ml/2 tsp cornflour (cornstarch)
5ml/1 tsp sugar
45ml/3 tbsp sunflower oil
50g/2oz/4 tbsp butter, melted

FOR THE SAUCE
150g/5oz/10 tbsp unsalted butter
5cm/2in cinnamon stick, broken up
3 cardamom pods, bruised
4 cloves
2 green chillies, roughly chopped
15ml/1 tbsp crushed fresh ginger
15ml/1 tbsp crushed garlic
5–10ml/1–2 tsp chilli powder
400g/14oz canned chopped tomatoes
30ml/2 tbsp tomato purée (paste)
10ml/2 tsp sugar
10ml/2 tsp salt
200ml/7fl oz/3/4 cup warm water
10ml/2 tsp dried fenugreek leaves
150ml/1/4 pint/1/2 cup double
    (heavy) cream

1 Rub the lemon juice and salt into the chicken. Whisk the yogurt and stir in the remaining tikka ingredients, except the melted butter. Stir into the chicken, cover and chill overnight.

2 Pre-heat the grill (broiler) to high. Thread the chicken on to oiled skewers and place on the grill pan. Cook for 5 minutes. Mix the marinade with melted butter. Brush over the chicken and cook for 3–4 minutes. Turn and baste. Cook for 2–3 minutes. Remove from the heat.

3 For the sauce, melt half the butter. Add the spices, chillies, ginger, garlic and chilli powder. Cook for 2–3 minutes. Add the remaining ingredients except the cream. Simmer for 20 minutes. Cool. Purée until smooth with a hand blender or sieve (strainer).

4 Return the pan to the heat, and add the remaining butter and cream. Let the mixture come to a simmer, then add the chicken. Simmer for 5–6 minutes, and serve with boiled rice.

Nutritional information per portion: Energy 793kcal/3293kJ; Protein 45.8g; Carbohydrate 14.2g, of which sugars 9g; Fat 64.4g, of which saturates 37.1g; Cholesterol 227mg; Calcium 102mg; Fibre 1.2g; Sodium 1491mg.

Creamy chicken korma

This classic chicken korma recipe calls for creamy coconut milk and chilli. Subtle flavours are added with cinnamon, cardamom and a little nutmeg and mace.

SERVES 4

50g/2oz/¹/₂ cup raw cashew nuts
200g/7oz/³/₄ cup thick set natural
   (plain) yogurt
10ml/2 tsp gram flour
10ml/2 tsp crushed fresh root ginger
10ml/2 tsp crushed garlic
2.5ml/¹/₂ tsp ground turmeric
2.5–5ml/1/2–1 tsp chilli powder
5ml/1 tsp salt, or to taste
675g/1¹/₂lb skinless chicken breast fillets,
   cut into 5cm/2in cubes

75g/3oz/6 tbsp ghee or unsalted butter
2.5cm/1in piece of cinnamon stick
6 green cardamom pods, bruised
6 cloves
2 bay leaves
1 large onion, finely chopped
15ml/1 tbsp sesame seeds, finely ground
200ml/7fl oz/³/₄ cup canned coconut milk
1.5ml/¹/₄ tsp freshly grated nutmeg
1.5ml/¹/₄ tsp ground mace
Indian bread or boiled basmati rice, to serve

1 Soak the cashew nuts in 150ml/¹/₄ pint/²/₃ cup boiling water for 20 minutes. Whisk the yogurt and gram flour together until smooth. Add the ginger, garlic, turmeric, chilli powder and salt. Mix well and stir into the chicken. Set aside for 30–35 minutes.

2 Reserve 5ml/1 tsp of ghee or butter and melt the remainder in a medium pan over a low heat. Add the cinnamon, cardamom, cloves and bay leaves. Stir-fry for 3–4 minutes.

3 Increase the heat and fry the onion until translucent. Stir in the ground sesame seeds and the chicken. Cook for 5 minutes. Add the coconut milk and 150ml/¹/₄ pint/²/₃ cup warm water. Bring to the boil, reduce the heat, cover and simmer for 20 minutes.

4 Meanwhile, purée the cashews with the water in which they were soaked and add to the chicken. Simmer, uncovered, for 5–6 minutes until the sauce thickens.

5 Melt the reserved ghee or butter in a pan over low heat. Add the nutmeg and mace, then cook gently for 30 seconds. Stir the spiced butter into the chicken. Serve with rice or bread.

Nutritional information per portion: Energy 398kcal/1671kJ; Protein 46.4g; Carbohydrate 19.1g, of which sugars 12.5g; Fat 16g, of which saturates 3.8g; Cholesterol 76mg; Calcium 195mg; Fibre 2.1g; Sodium 265mg.

Classic chicken curry

This recipe uses plenty of curry powder to give it a real bite. It is best served with plain boiled or steamed rice to moderate the spicy flavours.

SERVES 4

675g/1¹/₂lb chicken leg or breast joint
    pieces on the bone
2.5ml/¹/₂ tsp ground turmeric
15ml/1 tbsp plain (all-purpose) flour
5ml/1 tsp salt, or to taste
1 large onion, roughly chopped
2.5cm/1in piece of fresh root ginger,
    roughly chopped
4–5 garlic cloves, roughly chopped
60ml/4 tbsp sunflower oil or olive oil
25ml/1¹/₂ tbsp curry powder
2.5ml/¹/₂ tsp chilli powder (optional)
175g/6oz fresh tomatoes, peeled
    and chopped
30ml/2 tbsp chopped fresh
    coriander (cilantro)
plain boiled or steamed basmati rice,
    to serve

1 Skin the chicken and separate the legs from the thighs. For breast meat, cut each into three pieces. Mix the turmeric, flour and salt and rub the mixture into the chicken. Set aside in a cool place to marinate then prepare the other flavourings.

2 Put the onion, ginger and garlic in a food processor and purée; or you can pound them together into a paste using a mortar and pestle.

3 Heat the sunflower or olive oil in a medium pan and add the puréed ingredients. Cook over medium heat for 8–10 minutes, stirring regularly so that the paste does not burn.

4 Add the curry powder and chilli powder, if using, and cook for 2–3 minutes. Add about 30ml/2 tbsp water and continue to cook for a further 2–3 minutes.

5 Add the chicken, increase the heat to medium-high and stir until the chicken begins to brown. Add 425ml/15fl oz/1³/₄ cups warm water, bring it to the boil, cover and reduce the heat to low. Cook for another 35–40 minutes then add the tomatoes. Cook for 2–3 minutes, stir in the chopped coriander and remove the pan from the heat. Serve the curry with plain boiled or steamed rice.

Nutritional information per portion: Energy 392kcal/1632kJ; Protein 24.3g; Carbohydrate 12.5g, of which sugars 7.3g; Fat 27.6g, of which saturates 5.8g; Cholesterol 135mg; Calcium 67mg; Fibre 2.6g; Sodium 108mg.

Savoury chicken korma

There are many types of korma, and contrary to popular belief, a korma is not an actual dish, but a technique that is used in Indian cooking.

SERVES 4

675g/1¹/₂lb boned chicken thighs or breast fillets, skinned and cut into 5cm/2in pieces

75g/3oz/¹/₃ cup whole milk natural (plain) yogurt

10ml/2 tsp gram flour

5ml/1 tsp salt

10ml/2 tsp crushed fresh root ginger

10ml/2 tsp crushed garlic

60ml/4 tbsp ghee or unsalted butter

2.5cm/1in piece of cinnamon stick

1 large onion, finely sliced

2.5ml/¹/₂ tsp ground turmeric

15ml/1 tbsp ground coriander

2.5ml/¹/₂ tsp chilli powder, or to taste

50g/2oz/¹/₂ cup raw unsalted cashew nuts, soaked in boiling water for about 15 minutes

150ml/¹/₄ pint/²/₃ cup double (heavy) cream

2.5ml/¹/₂ tsp ground cardamom

2.5ml/¹/₂ tsp ground mace

1 Put the chicken in a large mixing bowl. Beat the yogurt and the gram flour together and add to the chicken. Add the salt, ginger and garlic, and mix well. Cover and leave to marinate for about an hour.

2 Heat the ghee or butter in a heavy pan over medium heat and add the cinnamon, followed by the onion. Stir-fry for 5–6 minutes until the onion is soft and translucent.

3 Add the turmeric, coriander and chilli powder, stir-fry for 1 minute, then add the chicken to the pan.

4 Increase the heat slightly and stir-fry the ingredients for about 3–4 minutes until the chicken begins to change colour. Pour in 300ml/¹/₂ pint/1¹/₄ cups warm water, bring it to the boil, reduce the heat to low, cover and simmer for 15 minutes.

5 Drain the soaked cashew nuts and purée them in a food processor or blender with the cream. Add to the chicken and simmer for 2–3 minutes. Stir in the ground cardamom and mace, remove from the heat and serve.

Nutritional information per portion: Energy 343kcal/1450kJ; Protein 54g; Carbohydrate 18g, of which sugars 10.7g; Fat 6.8g, of which saturates 2.6g; Cholesterol 151mg; Calcium 66mg; Fibre 1.8g; Sodium 197mg.

Chicken in golden saffron sauce

Saffron is said to be worth its weight in gold, and its characteristic bouquet adds a unique colour, aroma and flavour to this succulent dish.

SERVES 4

50g/2oz blanched almonds
675g/1¹/₂lb skinless, boneless chicken thighs or breast fillets, cubed
10ml/2 tsp crushed garlic
10ml/2 tsp crushed fresh root ginger
5ml/1 tsp ground cumin
7.5ml/1¹/₂ tsp ground coriander
2.5–5ml/¹/₂–1 tsp crushed dried chillies
1 large onion, finely chopped
75g/3oz/¹/₃ cup natural (plain) yogurt
10ml/2 tsp gram flour
4 each cloves and cardamom pods, split
2.5cm/1in piece of cinnamon stick
25g/1oz ghee or unsalted butter
300ml/¹/₂ pint/1¹/₄ cups milk
2.5ml/ tsp saffron strands, pounded and soaked in 15ml/1 tbsp hot milk
2.5ml/¹/₂ tsp garam masala
1–2 fresh green chillies, seeded and cut into julienne strips, to garnish

1 Soak the almonds in 150ml/¹/₄ pint/²/₃ cup boiling water for 20 minutes. Put the chicken, garlic, ginger, cumin, coriander, crushed chillies and onion in a heavy pan. Beat the yogurt and gram flour together and add to the pan. Add the cloves, cardamom pods and cinnamon, and place the pan over medium heat. Stir until the contents sizzle. Reduce the heat to low, cover the pan with a lid and cook for 20–25 minutes.

2 Remove the lid and increase the heat to high. Cook until the liquid is reduced to a thick batter-like consistency, stirring frequently. Add the ghee or butter and stir-fry the chicken for another 3–4 minutes until the fat rises to the surface.

3 Purée the almonds with the soaking water and add to the pan. Stir in the milk, the saffron and the soaking milk. Bring it to the boil. Reduce the heat and simmer for 5–6 minutes. Stir in the garam masala. Transfer to a serving dish and garnish with the green chilli. Serve immediately.

Nutritional information per portion: Energy 554kcal/2321kJ; Protein 75.6g; Carbohydrate 5.1g, of which sugars 4.7g; Fat 25.9g, of which saturates 12.2g; Cholesterol 255mg; Calcium 146mg; Fibre 0.8g; Sodium 792mg.

Curried chicken with shallots

This richly spiced dish makes a delectable main course for a light summer dinner when served with naan bread and a vegetable side dish.

SERVES 4

675g/1½lb skinned chicken thigh or
    breast fillets, cut into 5cm/2in cubes
juice of ½ lemon
5ml/1 tsp salt or to taste
60ml/4 tbsp sunflower oil
2 medium onions, finely chopped
15ml/1 tbsp each ginger and garlic purée
7.5ml/1½ tsp ground coriander
5ml/1 tsp each ground cumin and turmeric
2.5–5ml/½–1 tsp chilli powder
225g/8oz canned chopped tomatoes,
15ml/1 tbsp ghee
8–10 small whole shallots
2.5–5ml/½–1 tsp garam masala
15ml/1 tbsp chopped fresh mint
4–5 whole green chillies
10ml/2 tbsp chopped fresh coriander
    (cilantro) leaves
naan bread and a side dish, to serve

1 Put the chicken in a bowl and add the lemon juice and salt. Mix thoroughly, cover and set aside in a cool place for 30 minutes.

2 In a pan, heat the oil and sauté the onions, ginger and garlic over a medium heat for 7–8 minutes. Add the coriander, cumin, turmeric and chilli powder and cook gently for about 1 minute, then add the tomatoes. Cook, stirring, until the tomatoes reach a paste-like consistency and the oil separates from the paste. Increase the heat to high and add the chicken. Cook, stirring, for 4–5 minutes. Add 250ml/8fl oz/1 cup warm water, bring it to the boil and reduce the heat to low. Cover and cook for 15–20 minutes, stirring occasionally for even flavour.

3 In a separate pan, heat the ghee. Add the shallots and stir-fry until lightly browned, then add the garam masala. Add this mixture to the chicken and stir over a medium heat until thickened. Add the mint, chillies and chopped coriander. Mix and cook for 1–2 minutes. Serve with naan and a side dish.

Nutritional information per portion: Energy 401kcal/1678kJ; Protein 42.6g; Carbohydrate 18.2g, of which sugars 10.6g; Fat 18.3g, of which saturates 3.3g; Cholesterol 75mg; Calcium 99mg; Fibre 3.7g; Sodium 143mg.

Spiced Cambodian chicken curry

There are many recipes for Cambodian chicken or seafood curries, but the basic ingredients for the sauces are usually Indian curry powder and coconut milk.

SERVES 4

45ml/3 tbsp Indian curry powder or
   garam masala
15ml/1 tbsp ground turmeric
500g/1¼lb skinless chicken thighs or
   chicken portions
25ml/1½ tbsp raw cane sugar
30ml/2 tbsp sesame oil
2 shallots, chopped
2 garlic cloves, chopped
4cm/1½in galangal, peeled and chopped

2 lemon grass stalks, chopped
10ml/2 tsp chilli paste or dried chilli flakes
2 medium sweet potatoes, peeled
   and cubed
45ml/3 tbsp nuoc cham (Vietnamese
   fish sauce)
600ml/1 pint/2½ cups coconut milk
1 small bunch each fresh basil and coriander
   (cilantro), stalks removed
salt and ground black pepper

1 In a small bowl, mix together the curry powder or garam masala and the turmeric. Put the chicken in a bowl and coat with half of the spice. Set aside.

2 To make the caramel sauce, heat the sugar in a small pan with 7.5ml/1½ tsp water, until the sugar dissolves and the syrup turns golden. Remove from the heat and set aside.

3 Heat a wok or heavy pan and add the oil. Stir-fry the shallots, garlic, galangal and lemon grass.

4 Stir in the rest of the turmeric and curry powder or garam masala with the chilli paste or flakes, followed by the chicken, and cook for 2–3 minutes, stirring frequently.

5 Add the sweet potatoes, then the nuoc cham, caramel sauce, coconut milk and 150ml/¼ pint/²⁄₃ cup water, mixing thoroughly to combine the flavours. Bring to the boil, reduce the heat and cook for about 15 minutes until the chicken is cooked through.

6 Season and stir in half the fresh basil and coriander. Garnish with the remaining herbs and serve the curry immediately.

Nutritional information per portion: Energy 387kcal/1632kJ; Protein 31g; Carbohydrate 38g, of which sugars 19g; Fat 14g, of which saturates 3g; Cholesterol 131mg; Calcium 1.8mg; Fibre 1g; Sodium 1000mg.

Southern chicken curry

This is a mild coconut curry flavoured with turmeric, coriander, cumin seeds and shrimp paste, which demonstrates the influence of Malaysian cooking on Thai cuisine.

SERVES 4

60ml/4 tbsp vegetable oil
1 large garlic clove, crushed
1 chicken, weighing about 1.5kg/
   3–3^1/$_2$lb, chopped into
   12 large pieces
400ml/14fl oz/1^2/$_3$ cups
   coconut cream
250ml/8fl oz/1 cup chicken stock
30ml/2 tbsp Thai fish sauce
30ml/2 tbsp sugar
juice of 2 limes

FOR THE CURRY PASTE

5ml/1 tsp dried chilli flakes
2.5ml/^{1}/$_2$ tsp salt
5cm/2in piece fresh turmeric or 5ml/1 tsp
   ground turmeric
2.5ml/^{1}/$_2$ tsp coriander seeds
2.5ml/^{1}/$_2$ tsp cumin seeds
5ml/1 tsp dried shrimp paste

TO GARNISH

2 small fresh red chillies, seeded
   and chopped
1 bunch spring onions (scallions), sliced

1 For the curry paste, put all the ingredients in a mortar, food processor or spice grinder and pound, process or grind to a smooth paste.

2 Heat the oil in a wok or large frying pan and cook the garlic until golden. Add the chicken and cook until golden on all sides. Remove the chicken and set aside.

3 Reheat the oil and add the curry paste and then half the coconut cream. Cook, stirring, for a few minutes until fragrant.

4 Return the chicken to the wok or pan, add the stock, mixing well, then add the remaining coconut cream, the fish sauce, sugar and lime juice. Stir well and bring to the boil, then lower the heat and simmer for 15 minutes.

5 Turn the curry into four warm serving bowls and sprinkle with the chopped fresh chillies and spring onions to garnish. Serve immediately.

Nutritional information per portion: Energy 612Kcal/2541kJ; Protein 38.5g; Carbohydrate 9g, of which sugars 8.9g; Fat 47.1g, of which saturates 26.4g; Cholesterol 139mg; Calcium 22mg; Fibre 0g; Sodium 447mg.

Ethiopian curried chicken

The long-simmered stews eaten in Ethiopia are known as wats. This delectable curry is made in a slow cooker to replicate the traditional techniques used in making wats.

SERVES 4

30ml/2 tbsp vegetable oil
2 large onions, chopped
3 garlic cloves, chopped
2.5cm/1in piece peeled and finely
   chopped fresh root ginger
175ml/6fl oz/³/₄ cup chicken or
   vegetable stock
400g/14oz can chopped tomatoes
seeds from 5 cardamom pods
2.5ml/¹/₂ tsp ground turmeric
large pinch of ground cinnamon
large pinch of ground cloves
large pinch of grated nutmeg
1.3kg/3lb chicken, cut into 8–12 portions
4 hard-boiled eggs
cayenne pepper or hot paprika, to taste
salt and ground black pepper
chopped fresh coriander (cilantro) and
   onion rings, to garnish
flatbread or rice, to serve

1 Heat the oil in a large pan, add the onions and cook for 10 minutes until softened. Add the garlic and ginger to the pan and cook for 1–2 minutes.

2 Add the stock and the chopped tomatoes to the pan. Bring to the boil and cook, stirring frequently, for about 10 minutes, or until the mixture has thickened, then season.

3 Transfer the mixture to a ceramic cooking pot and stir in the cardamom seeds, turmeric, cinnamon, cloves and nutmeg. Add the chicken in a single layer, pushing the pieces well down so that they are covered by the sauce. Cover the slow cooker with the lid and cook on high for 3 hours.

4 Remove the shells from the eggs, then prick the eggs a few times with a fork or very fine skewer. Add to the sauce and cook for 30–45 minutes, or until the chicken is cooked through and tender. Season to taste with cayenne pepper or hot paprika. Garnish with the fresh coriander and onion rings and serve immediately with flatbread or rice.

Nutritional information per portion: Energy 388kcal/1629kJ; Protein 54.6g; Carbohydrate 13g, of which sugars 9.6g; Fat 13.4g, of which saturates 2.8g; Cholesterol 13mg; Calcium 81mg; Fibre 2.5g; Sodium 311mg.

Spicy chicken in cashew nut sauce

This mildly spiced, slow-cooker dish has a rich yet delicately flavoured sauce, owing to the addition of cashew nuts and yogurt. Sultanas add a hint of sweetness to the curry.

SERVES 4

1 large onion, roughly chopped
1 garlic clove, crushed
15ml/1 tbsp tomato purée (paste)
50g/2oz/¹/₂ cup cashew nuts
7.5ml/1¹/₂ tsp garam masala
5ml/1 tsp chilli powder
1.5ml/¹/₄ tsp ground turmeric
5ml/1 tsp salt
15ml/1 tbsp lemon juice
15ml/1 tbsp natural (plain) yogurt
30ml/2 tbsp vegetable oil
450g/1lb chicken breast fillets, skinned
    and cubed
175g/6oz/2¹/₄ cups button
    (white) mushrooms
15ml/1 tbsp sultanas (golden raisins)
300ml/¹/₂ pint/1¹/₄ cups chicken
    or vegetable stock
30ml/2 tbsp chopped fresh coriander
    (cilantro), plus extra to garnish
rice and fruit chutney, to serve

1 Put the onion, garlic, tomato purée, cashew nuts, garam masala, chilli powder, turmeric, salt, lemon juice and yogurt in a food processor and process to a paste.

2 Heat the oil in a large frying pan or wok and fry the cubes of chicken for a few minutes, or until just beginning to brown. Using a slotted spoon, transfer the chicken to a ceramic cooking pot, leaving the oil in the pan. Add the spice paste and mushrooms to the pan, lower the heat and fry gently, stirring frequently, for 3–4 minutes. Transfer the mixture to the ceramic pot.

3 Add the sultanas to the pot and stir in the chicken or vegetable stock. Cover with the lid and switch the slow cooker to high. Cook for 3–4 hours, stirring halfway through the cooking time. The chicken should be cooked through and very tender, and the sauce fairly thick.

4 Add the chopped coriander, then season to taste, if necessary. Serve the curry from the ceramic cooking pot or a warmed serving dish and garnish with fresh coriander. Serve with rice and a fruit chutney, such as mango.

Nutritional information per portion: Energy 239kcal/1006kJ; Protein 31.6g; Carbohydrate 10.7g, of which sugars 7.6g; Fat 8.1g, of which saturates 1.7g; Cholesterol 78.9mg; Calcium 39mg; Fibre 1.9g; Sodium 696mg.

Gochujang chicken stew

This is a warming chicken stew with vegetables and spices. Chillies and gochujang chilli paste supply a vivid red colour and give the chicken a fiery quality. With a delicious hint of sweetness offsetting the piquancy, this is the perfect hearty meal for chilly evenings. Keep accompanying dishes simple, ideally just steamed rice and a side dish.

SERVES 4

3 potatoes, peeled
1 carrot, peeled
2 onions, peeled
1 chicken, about 800g/1¾lb
30ml/2 tbsp vegetable oil
2 garlic cloves, crushed
3 green chillies, seeded and finely sliced
1 red chilli, seeded and finely sliced
15ml/1 tbsp sesame oil
salt and ground black pepper
2 spring onions (scallions), finely chopped,
   to garnish

FOR THE MARINADE

30ml/2 tbsp mirin or rice wine
salt and ground black pepper

FOR THE SEASONING

15ml/1 tbsp sesame seeds
10ml/2 tsp light soy sauce
30ml/2 tbsp gochujang chilli paste
45ml/3 tbsp Korean chilli powder

1 Cut the potatoes into bitesize pieces. Soak in cold water for 15–20 minutes and drain. Cut the carrot and onions into medium-size pieces.

2 Cut the chicken, with skin and bone, into bitesize pieces and place in a dish with the marinade ingredients. Stir to coat and leave for 10 minutes.

3 Heat 15ml/1 tbsp vegetable oil in a frying pan or wok, and quickly stir-fry the crushed garlic. Add the chicken and stir-fry, draining off any fat that comes from the meat during cooking. When lightly browned, place the chicken on kitchen paper to remove any excess oil.

4 To make the seasoning, grind the sesame seeds in a mortar and pestle. Combine the soy sauce, gochujang paste, chilli powder and ground sesame seeds in a bowl.

5 In a pan, heat the remaining vegetable oil and add the potatoes, carrot and onions. Briefly cook over medium heat, stirring well, and then add the chicken.

6 Pour over enough water to cover two-thirds of the meat and vegetables. Bring to the boil. Add the seasoning and reduce the heat. Stir the seasoning into the water and simmer until the volume of liquid has reduced by about one-third.

7 Add the green and red sliced chillies to the stew, then simmer for a little longer, stirring constantly until the liquid has thickened slightly.

8 Add the sesame oil, season with salt and ground black pepper, then transfer to deep serving bowls and garnish with the chopped spring onion before serving.

Nutritional information per portion: Energy 470kcal/1955kJ; Protein 27.4g; Carbohydrate 20.4g, of which sugars 4.7g; Fat 31.5g, of which saturates 7.5g; Cholesterol 128mg; Calcium 56mg; Fibre 2.3g; Sodium 296mg.

Chicken coconut stew

In this recipe, chicken on the bone is cooked in a rich coconut broth. In south-west India, it is served with 'appam', a plain rice flour pancake, but it is also good with plain boiled basmati rice.

SERVES 4

675g/1½lb chicken leg or breast joints
   on the bone
60ml/4 tbsp sunflower oil or olive oil
2.5cm/1in piece of cinnamon stick
6 cardamom pods, bruised
4 cloves
12–15 curry leaves
1 large onion, finely chopped
10ml/2 tsp ginger purée
10ml/2 tsp garlic purée
2 green chillies, sliced at an angle
2.5ml/½ tsp ground turmeric
400g/14fl oz/1½ cups canned
   coconut milk
5ml/1 tsp salt, or to taste
500g/1¼lb medium potatoes
175g/6oz/1½ cups frozen garden peas
plain boiled basmati rice, to serve

1 Skin the chicken joints, and cut each one into two pieces, then set them aside.

2 Heat the oil in a large pan over a low heat and add the cinnamon, cardamom pods, cloves and curry leaves. Sauté for 25–30 seconds and add the onion. Increase the heat to medium and fry until the onion is soft, about 5–6 minutes.

3 Add the ginger, garlic and chillies and cook for 2–3 minutes longer. Add the turmeric, stir well, then add the chicken. Increase the heat from medium to high and stir until the chicken browns.

4 Pour in the coconut milk and add the salt, stir and mix well. Reduce the heat to low, cover and simmer for 15–20 minutes.

5 Halve the potatoes, add to the stew and pour in 250ml/8fl oz/1 cup warm water. Bring to the boil, reduce the heat to low, then cover the pan and cook the stew for an additional 20 minutes, or until the chicken is cooked and the potatoes are tender.

6 Add the frozen peas, cook for about 5 minutes longer and remove from the heat. Serve with plain boiled basmati rice.

Nutritional information per portion: Energy 552kcal/2309kJ; Protein 40g; Carbohydrate 43.6g, of which sugars 16g; Fat 25.5g, of which saturates 6.9g; Cholesterol 192.5mg; Calcium 104.5mg; Fibre 5.4g; Sodium 271mg.

Yellow chicken and papaya

The pairing of slightly sweet coconut milk and fruit with savoury chicken and spices is a comforting, refreshing and exotic combination.

SERVES 4

300ml/¹⁄₂ pint/1¹⁄₄ cups chicken stock
30ml/2 tbsp thick tamarind juice, made
   by mixing tamarind paste with
   warm water
15ml/1 tbsp sugar
200ml/7fl oz/scant 1 cup coconut milk
1 green papaya, peeled, seeded and
   thinly sliced
250g/9oz skinless chicken breast
   fillets, diced
juice of 1 lime
lime slices, to garnish

FOR THE CURRY PASTE

1 fresh red chilli, seeded and chopped
4 garlic cloves, coarsely chopped
3 shallots, coarsely chopped
2 lemon grass stalks, sliced
5cm/2in piece fresh turmeric, coarsely
   chopped, or 5ml/1 tsp ground turmeric
5ml/1 tsp shrimp paste
5ml/1 tsp salt

1 Make the paste. Put the red chilli, garlic, shallots, lemon grass and turmeric in a mortar or food processor. Add the shrimp paste and salt. Pound or process to a paste.

2 Pour the stock into a wok or large saucepan and bring it to the boil. Stir in the curry paste.

3 Return to the boil and add the tamarind juice, sugar and coconut milk. Add the papaya and chicken to the pan and cook over medium to high heat for about 10–15 minutes, stirring frequently, until the chicken is cooked through. Stir in the lime juice, transfer to a warm dish and serve, garnished with lime slices.

Nutritional information per portion: Energy 125kcal/533kJ; Protein 15.7g; Carbohydrate 52.8g, of which sugars 51.5g; Fat 7.5g, of which saturates 1.2g; Cholesterol 79mg; Calcium 92mg; Fibre 2.6g; Sodium 150mg.

Spiced coconut chicken with cardamom, chilli and ginger

The chicken legs are marinated overnight in an aromatic blend of yogurt and spices before gently simmering with hot green chillies in creamy coconut milk. Serve with rice or Indian breads.

SERVES 4

1.6kg/3½ lb large chicken drumsticks
30ml/2 tbsp sunflower oil
400ml/14fl oz/1⅔ cups coconut milk
4–6 large green chillies, halved
45ml/3 tbsp chopped coriander (cilantro)
salt and ground black pepper
natural (plain) yogurt, to drizzle, optional

FOR THE MARINADE

15ml/1 tbsp crushed cardamom seeds
15ml/1 tbsp grated fresh root ginger
10ml/2 tsp finely grated garlic
105ml/7 tbsp natural (plain) yogurt
2 green chillies, seeded and chopped
5ml/1 tsp ground cumin
5ml/1 tsp ground coriander
5ml/1 tsp turmeric
finely grated zest and juice of 1 lime

1 Make the marinade. Place the cardamom, ginger, garlic, half the yogurt, green chillies, cumin, coriander, turmeric and lime zest and juice in a blender. Process until smooth, season and pour into a bowl.

2 Add the chicken drumsticks to the marinade and toss to coat evenly. Cover the bowl and marinate in the refrigerator overnight.

3 Heat the oil in a large wok over a low heat. Remove the chicken from the marinade, reserving the marinade.

4 Add the chicken to the wok and brown all over, then add the coconut milk, remaining yogurt, reserved marinade and green chillies and bring to a boil.

5 Reduce the heat and simmer gently, uncovered, for about 30–35 minutes. Check the seasoning, adding more salt and pepper if needed. Stir in the coriander, ladle into warmed bowls and serve immediately. Drizzle the chicken with yogurt, if liked.

Nutritional information per portion: Energy 706kcal/2935kJ; Protein 48.1g; Carbohydrate 15.8g, of which sugars 15.6g; Fat 50.4g, of which saturates 12.8g; Cholesterol 240mg; Calcium 91mg; Fibre 1.5g; Sodium 305mg.

Spicy chicken and pork cooked with vinegar and ginger

This dish can be made with chicken, with pork or with both, as in this recipe. It is a versatile recipe that can also be prepared with fish, shellfish and vegetables.

SERVES 4–6

30ml/2 tbsp groundnut (peanut) oil

6–8 garlic cloves, crushed whole

50g/2oz fresh root ginger, sliced into matchsticks

6 spring onions (scallions), cut into 2.5cm/1in pieces

5–10ml/1–2 tsp whole black peppercorns, crushed

30ml/2 tbsp palm (jaggery) or muscovado (molasses) sugar

8–10 chicken thighs and drumsticks

350g/12oz pork tenderloin (fillet), cut into chunks

150ml/¼ pint/⅔ cup coconut vinegar

150ml/¼ pint/⅔ cup dark soy sauce

300ml/½ pint/1¼ cups chicken stock

2–3 bay leaves

salt

TO SERVE

stir-fried greens and cooked rice

1 Heat the oil in a wok with a lid, stir in the garlic and ginger and fry until fragrant and they begin to colour. Add the spring onions and black pepper and stir in the sugar. Add the chicken and pork to the wok or casserole and fry until they begin to colour. Pour in the vinegar, soy sauce and chicken stock. Add the bay leaves.

2 Bring to the boil, reduce the heat to low, cover and simmer gently for about 1 hour, until the meat is tender and the liquid has reduced.

3 Season with salt and serve with stir-fried greens and plain boiled rice. Add some of the cooking liquid to each serving.

Nutritional information per portion: Energy 270kcal/1135kJ; Protein 42.2g; Carbohydrate 9g, of which sugars 7.6g; Fat 7.4g, of which saturates 1.6g; Cholesterol 118mg; Calcium 24mg; Fibre 0.6g; Sodium 1892mg.

Green chicken curry

You can vary the number of chillies in this delectable dish, adding more or fewer, depending on how hot you prefer your curry. Coconut rice is a soothing contrast to serve with this spicy curry.

SERVES 3–4

4 spring onions (scallions), trimmed and
    coarsely chopped
1–2 fresh green chillies, seeded and
    coarsely chopped
2cm/³⁄₄in piece fresh root ginger, peeled
2 garlic cloves
5ml/1 tsp fish sauce
large bunch fresh coriander (cilantro),
    roughly chopped
small handful of fresh parsley,
    roughly chopped
30–45ml/2–3 tbsp water
30ml/2 tbsp sunflower oil
4 skinless chicken breast fillets, diced
1 green (bell) pepper, seeded and
    thinly sliced
600ml/1 pint/2¹⁄₂ cups coconut milk
salt and ground black pepper
coconut rice, to serve (*see* page 164)

1 Put the spring onions, chillies, ginger, garlic, fish sauce and herbs in a food processor or blender. Pour in about 30ml/2 tbsp of the water and process to a smooth paste, adding more water if the mixture is a little dry.

2 Heat half the oil in a large frying pan. Cook the diced chicken until evenly browned. Transfer to a plate. Heat the remaining oil in the pan. Add the green pepper and stir-fry for 3–4 minutes. Add the chilli and ginger paste to the pan. Stir-fry for a further 3–4 minutes, until the mixture becomes fairly thick.

3 Return the chicken to the pan and add the coconut milk. Season with salt and pepper and bring to the boil, reduce the heat, half cover the pan and simmer for 8–10 minutes. When the chicken is cooked, transfer it, with the green pepper, to a plate. Boil the cooking liquid remaining in the pan for 10–12 minutes, until it is well reduced and fairly thick.

4 Return the chicken and pepper to the sauce, stir well and cook gently for 2–3 minutes. Spoon the curry over the coconut rice, and serve immediately.

Nutritional information per portion: Energy 208kcal/877kJ; Protein 28g; Carbohydrate 8g, of which sugars 7.9g; Fat 7.4g, of which saturates 1.3g; Cholesterol 79mg; Calcium 76mg; Fibre 0.7g; Sodium 237mg.

Fruity chicken and vegetable curry

Coconut milk creates a rich sauce for this dish that is sweet with fruit and fragrant with a spicy mixture of fresh herbs and spices, with an added kick from the chillies.

SERVES 4

4 garlic cloves, chopped
15ml/1 tbsp chopped fresh root ginger
2–3 chillies, chopped
bunch fresh coriander (cilantro) chopped
1 onion, chopped
juice of 1 lemon
2.5ml/½ tsp each curry powder and cumin
pinch of ground cloves, coriander and salt
3 skinless chicken thighs, cubed
30ml/2 tbsp vegetable oil
2 cinnamon sticks
250ml/8fl oz/1 cup chicken stock
250ml/8fl oz/1 cup coconut milk
15–30ml/1–2 tbsp sugar
1–2 bananas
¼ pineapple, peeled and chopped
small handful of sultanas (golden raisins)
2–3 sprigs of mint, thinly sliced
juice of ¼–½ lemon
flat bread, to serve

1 Purée the garlic, ginger, chillies, fresh coriander, onion, lemon juice, curry powder, cumin, cloves, ground coriander and salt in a food processor or blender. Toss together the chicken pieces with about 15–30ml/1–2 tbsp of the spice mixture and set aside.

2 Heat the oil in a wok or frying pan, then add the remaining spice mixture and cook over medium heat, stirring, for 10 minutes, or until the paste is lightly browned. Stir the cinnamon sticks, stock, coconut milk and sugar into the pan, bring to the boil, then simmer for 10 minutes.

3 Stir the chicken into the sauce and cook for 3–4 minutes, or until the chicken is nearly cooked through.

4 Meanwhile, thickly slice the bananas. Stir all the fruit into the pan and cook for 1–2 minutes. Add the mint and lemon juice. Remove the cinnamon sticks and serve immediately, with flat bread.

Nutritional information per portion: Energy 383kcal/1622kJ; Protein 29.5g; Carbohydrate 11.9g, of which sugars 11.7g; Fat 10.4g, of which saturates 2g; Cholesterol 140mg; Calcium 78mg; Fibre 1.1g; Sodium 462mg.

Red chicken curry with bamboo shoots

Bamboo shoots have a lovely crunchy texture and are great in curries. Fresh bamboo is not readily available in the West. When buying the canned variety, choose whole bamboo shoots, which are crisper and of better quality than sliced shoots.

SERVES 4–6

1 litre/1³⁄4 pints/4 cups coconut milk

450g/1lb skinless, boneless chicken
    breast portions, diced

30ml/2 tbsp Thai fish sauce

15ml/1 tbsp granulated (white) sugar

1–2 drained canned bamboo shoots,
    about 225g/8oz, rinsed and sliced

5 kaffir lime leaves, torn

salt and ground black pepper

chopped fresh red chillies and kaffir lime
    leaves, to garnish

FOR THE RED CURRY PASTE

5ml/1 tsp coriander seeds

2.5ml/¹⁄2 tsp cumin seeds

12–15 fresh red chillies, seeded
    and coarsely chopped

4 shallots, thinly sliced

2 garlic cloves, chopped

15ml/1 tbsp chopped
    fresh galangal

2 lemon grass stalks, chopped

3 kaffir lime leaves, chopped

4 fresh coriander (cilantro) roots

10 black peppercorns

good pinch ground cinnamon

5ml/1 tsp ground turmeric

2.5ml/¹⁄2 tsp shrimp paste

5ml/1 tsp salt

30ml/2 tbsp vegetable oil

1 Make the curry paste. Dry-fry the coriander seeds and cumin seeds for 1–2 minutes, then put in a mortar or food processor with the remaining ingredients except the oil. Pound or process to a paste.

2 Add the vegetable oil, a little at a time, mixing or processing well after each addition. Transfer to a screw-top jar, put on the lid and keep in the refrigerator until ready to use.

3 Pour half of the coconut milk into a large, heavy pan. Bring to the boil over a medium heat, stirring constantly until the coconut milk has separated.

4 Stir in 30ml/2 tbsp of the red curry paste and cook the mixture, stirring constantly, for 2–3 minutes, until the curry paste is thoroughly incorporated. The remaining red curry paste can be kept in the closed jar in the refrigerator for up to 3 months.

5 Add the chicken, fish sauce and sugar to the pan. Stir well, lower the heat and cook gently for 5–6 minutes, stirring to avoid sticking, until the chicken changes colour and is cooked through.

6 Pour the remaining coconut milk into the pan, then add the sliced bamboo shoots and torn lime leaves. Bring back to the boil over a medium heat, stirring constantly to prevent the mixture from sticking to the pan, then taste and add salt and pepper if necessary.

7 To serve, spoon the curry into a warmed serving dish and garnish with the chopped chillies and lime leaves.

Nutritional information per portion: Energy 255Kcal/1077kJ; Protein 29.5g; Carbohydrate 18g, of which sugars 16.9g; Fat 7.8g, of which saturates 1.5g; Cholesterol 79mg; Calcium 92mg; Fibre 0.9g; Sodium 1104mg.

Hot chicken curry

In this curry, with its deliciously spicy coating, the heat of the chillies is balanced by the addition of sweet onion, yogurt and shredded coconut.

SERVES 4

1.1kg/2¹/₂lb skinless chicken joints
115g/4oz/¹/₂ cup natural (plain) yogurt
10ml/2 tsp gram flour
5ml/1 tsp ground turmeric
5ml/1 tsp salt or to taste
25g/1oz/¹/₃ cup desiccated (dry
   unsweetened shredded) coconut
1 large onion, roughly chopped
2.5cm/1in piece of fresh root ginger, chopped
5 large garlic cloves, chopped
60ml/4 tbsp sunflower or olive oil
5cm/2in piece of cinnamon stick, halved
6 green cardamom pods, bruised

6 cloves
5–10ml/1–2 tsp chilli powder
2.5ml/¹/₂ tsp ground black pepper
115g/4oz chopped canned tomatoes, with
   their juice
2.5ml/¹/₂ tsp garam masala
15ml/1 tbsp chopped fresh coriander
   (cilantro) leaves
1 small tomato, seeded and cut into julienne
   strips, to garnish
1–2 green chillies, seeded and cut into
   julienne strips, to garnish
plain boiled rice, to serve

1 Cut each chicken joint into two pieces by separating the leg from the thigh and cutting each breast joint in half. In a large mixing bowl, whisk the yogurt with the gram flour, then add the turmeric and salt. Mix in the chicken and set aside for 1 hour.

2 In a heavy pan, dry-roast the coconut over a medium heat until lightly browned. Cool and grind in a blender.

3 Purée the onion, ginger and garlic in a food processor. Heat the oil and add the cinnamon, cardamom and cloves. Stir-fry for 2–3 minutes, then add the onion, ginger and garlic paste. Cook until the mixture begins to brown. Add the chilli powder and black pepper, and cook for 3 minutes.

4 Add the chicken and stir-fry for 3–4 minutes. Add the tomatoes and 200ml/7fl oz/scant 1 cup warm water. Bring to the boil, reduce the heat, cover and cook until the chicken is tender. Stir in the coconut and cook for 4–5 minutes. Stir in the garam masala and coriander. Remove from the heat. Transfer to a dish, garnish with tomato and chilli, and serve with rice.

Nutritional information per portion: Energy 605kcal/2508kJ; Protein 37.8g; Carbohydrate 13.8g, of which sugars 8.9g; Fat 44.7g, of which saturates 13.2g; Cholesterol 176.2mg; Calcium 107.8mg; Fibre 2.5g; Sodium 170mg.

Chicken and lemon grass curry

This tasty curry, with its characteristic mix of Thai flavourings: lemon grass, kaffir lime leaves and fish sauce, has a wonderful tangy aroma, and it is quick and simple to prepare.

SERVES 4

45ml/3 tbsp vegetable oil

2 garlic cloves, crushed

500g/1¼lb skinless, boneless chicken
thighs, diced

45ml/3 tbsp fish sauce

120ml/4fl oz/½ cup chicken stock

5ml/1 tsp sugar

1 lemon grass stalk, chopped and crushed

5 kaffir lime leaves, peanuts and fresh
coriander leaves, to garnish

FOR THE CURRY PASTE

1 lemon grass stalk, coarsely chopped

2.5cm/1in piece galangal, peeled and sliced

2 each kaffir lime leaves and shallots, sliced

3 shallots, coarsely chopped

6 coriander (cilantro) roots, chopped

2 garlic cloves

2 fresh green chillies, seeded and chopped

5ml/1 tsp shrimp paste

5ml/1 tsp ground turmeric

roasted peanuts and coriander (cilantro)

1 First make the curry paste. Place all the ingredients in a large mortar or food processor and pound with a pestle or process to a smooth paste.

2 Heat the vegetable oil in a wok, add the garlic and cook over low heat, stirring frequently, until golden brown. Be careful not to let the garlic burn or it will taste bitter.

3 Add the curry paste to the pan and cook for a further 30 seconds, stirring constantly.

4 Add the chicken pieces to the pan and stir until they are thoroughly coated with the curry paste. Stir in the fish sauce and chicken stock, then add the sugar, and cook, stirring constantly, for 2 minutes more.

5 Add the lemon grass and lime leaves, reduce the heat and simmer for 10 minutes. Chop a few roasted peanuts and fresh coriander leaves for garnish. Spoon the curry into four warmed dishes, garnish and serve immediately.

Nutritional information per portion: Energy 122kcal/512kJ; Protein 17.4g; Carbohydrate 3.7g, of which sugars 3g; Fat 4.3g, of which saturates 0.8g; Cholesterol 85mg; Calcium 77mg; Fibre 1.6g; Sodium 131mg.

Fragrant chicken curry

This classic red Thai curry is perfect for a party since the chicken and sauce can be prepared in advance and combined and heated at the last minute.

SERVES 4

45ml/3 tbsp vegetable oil
1 onion, coarsely chopped
2 garlic cloves, crushed
15ml/1 tbsp Thai red curry paste
115g/4oz creamed coconut dissolved in
    900ml/1½ pints/3¾ cups boiling
    water, or 1 litre/1¾ pints/4 cups
    coconut milk
2 lemon grass stalks, coarsely chopped
6 kaffir lime leaves, chopped
150ml/¼ pint/⅔ cup Greek
    (US strained plain) yogurt
30ml/2 tbsp apricot jam
1 cooked chicken, about 1.5kg/3–3½lb
30ml/2 tbsp chopped fresh
    coriander (cilantro)
salt and ground black pepper
kaffir lime leaves, shredded, toasted
    shredded coconut and fresh coriander
    (cilantro), to garnish
plain boiled rice, to serve

1 Heat the oil in a large pan. Add the onion and garlic and cook over low heat for 5–10 minutes until soft. Stir in the red curry paste. Cook, stirring constantly, for 2–3 minutes. Stir in the diluted creamed coconut or coconut milk, then add the lemon grass, lime leaves, yogurt and apricot jam. Stir well. Cover and simmer for 30 minutes.

2 Remove from the heat and cool slightly. Transfer the sauce to a food processor or blender and process to a purée, then strain it back into the rinsed-out pan, pressing as much of the puréed mixture as possible through the sieve (strainer) with the back of a wooden spoon. Set aside while you prepare the chicken.

3 Remove the skin from the chicken and discard, slice the meat off the bones and cut it into bitesize pieces. Add to the sauce. Bring the curry sauce back to simmering point. Stir in the chopped fresh coriander and season with salt and black pepper. Garnish with extra lime leaves, toasted shredded coconut and coriander. Serve immediately with rice, sprinkled with coriander leaves and black pepper.

Nutritional information per portion: Energy 837kcal/3472kJ; Protein 50.2g; Carbohydrate 14.2g, of which sugars 13.7g; Fat 64.6g, of which saturates 29.2g; Cholesterol 253mg; Calcium 85mg; Fibre 0.3g; Sodium 240mg.

Thai chicken curry

This is a flavourful and fragrant Thai curry with a lovely creamy taste owing to the addition of coconut milk. It is easy to make so will be ideal for a quick midweek meal for the whole family.

SERVES 6

400ml/14oz can coconut milk
6 skinless chicken breast fillets, sliced
225g/8oz can bamboo shoots, drained
    and sliced
30ml/2 tbsp Thai fish sauce
15ml/1 tbsp soft light brown sugar
cooked jasmine rice, to serve

FOR THE GREEN CURRY PASTE

4 fresh green chillies, seeded
1 lemon grass stalk, sliced
1 small onion, sliced
3 garlic cloves
1cm/$\frac{1}{2}$in piece fresh root ginger, peeled
grated rind of $\frac{1}{2}$ lime
5ml/1 tsp coriander seeds
5ml/1 tsp cumin seeds
2.5ml/$\frac{1}{2}$ tsp Thai fish sauce

TO GARNISH

1 fresh red chilli, seeded, cut into strips
finely pared rind of $\frac{1}{2}$ lime, shredded
fresh Thai purple basil or coriander
    (cilantro), chopped

1 First make the green curry paste: put all the ingredients in a food processor or blender and process to a thick paste. Set aside while you prepare the rest of the dish.

2 Bring half the coconut milk to the boil in a large frying pan, reduce the heat and simmer for 5 minutes, or until reduced by half. Stir in the green curry paste and simmer for 5 minutes. Add the chicken to the pan with the remaining coconut milk, bamboo shoots, fish sauce and sugar.

3 Stir well to combine all the ingredients then bring the curry back to simmering point, and simmer gently for about 10 minutes, or until the chicken slices are tender and cooked through. The mixture will look grainy or curdled during cooking but this is quite normal and is nothing to worry about.

4 Spoon the curry and rice into six warmed bowls, garnish with the chilli, lime rind, and basil or coriander, and serve immediately.

Nutritional information per portion: Energy 236kcal/991kJ; Protein 33.8g; Carbohydrate 7.2g, of which sugars 5.9g; Fat 8.3g, of which saturates 1.6g; Cholesterol 165mg; Calcium 149mg; Fibre 3.1g; Sodium 253mg.

Chicken with basil and chilli

This quick and easy chicken dish is an excellent introduction to cooking with chillies. Thai basil, sometimes known as holy basil, has a pungent flavour that is spicy and sharp.

SERVES 4–6

45ml/3 tbsp vegetable oil
4 garlic cloves, thinly sliced
2–4 fresh red chillies, seeded and finely chopped
450g/1lb skinless boneless chicken breast fillets, cut into bitesize pieces
45ml/3 tbsp Thai fish sauce
10ml/2 tsp dark soy sauce
5ml/1 tsp sugar
10–12 fresh Thai basil leaves
2 fresh red chillies, seeded and finely chopped, and about 20 deep-fried Thai basil leaves, to garnish

1 Heat the oil in a wok or large frying pan. Add the garlic and chillies and stir-fry for 1–2 minutes until the garlic is golden. Take care not to let the garlic burn, otherwise it will taste bitter.

2 Add the pieces of chicken to the wok or pan, in batches if necessary, and stir-fry until the chicken changes colour.

3 Stir in the fish sauce, soy sauce and sugar. Stir-fry the mixture for 3–4 minutes, or until the chicken is cooked through and golden brown in colour.

4 Stir in the fresh Thai basil leaves. Spoon the mixture on to a warm platter. Garnish with the chopped chillies and deep-fried Thai basil leaves and serve immediately.

Nutritional information per portion: Energy 214kcal/899kJ; Protein 28g; Carbohydrate 4g, of which sugars 10g; Fat 10g, of which saturates 1g; Cholesterol 79mg; Calcium 14mg; Fibre 0.1g; Sodium 700mg.

Curry kapitan with coconut and chilli relish

Curry Kapitan recalls the traditional role of the Chinese Kapitan, a man of considerable social standing among the Malay and Chinese people in old Melaka. It is thought to be a dish that was invented to present to the Kapitan or to celebrate his role. A chicken curry, made with coconut milk, it spans the spectrum of the inhabitants of old Melaka through its use of spices and flavourings – Chinese, Malay, Portuguese and Indian.

SERVES 4

FOR THE REMPAH SPICE PASTE

6–8 dried red chillies, soaked in warm water
   until soft, seeded and squeezed dry
6–8 shallots, chopped
4–6 garlic cloves, chopped
25g/1oz fresh root ginger, chopped
5ml/1 tsp shrimp paste
10ml/2 tsp ground turmeric
10ml/2 tsp Chinese five-spice powder

FOR THE CURRY

15–30ml/1–2 tbsp tamarind pulp
1 fresh coconut, grated (shredded)
30–45ml/2–3 tbsp vegetable or groundnut
   (peanut) oil

1–2 cinnamon sticks
12 chicken thighs, boned and cut into bitesize
   strips lengthways
600ml/1 pint/2$\frac{1}{2}$ cups coconut milk
15ml/1 tbsp palm sugar
salt and ground black pepper

FOR THE RELISH

1 green chilli, seeded and finely sliced
1 red chilli, seeded and finely sliced
fresh coriander (cilantro) leaves, finely
   chopped (reserve a few leaves for
   garnishing)
2 limes
steamed rice, to serve

1 First make the rempah. Using a mortar and pestle or food processor, grind the chillies, shallots, garlic and ginger to a paste. Beat in the shrimp paste and stir in the dried spices.

2 Soak the tamarind pulp in 150ml/$\frac{1}{4}$ pint/$\frac{2}{3}$ cup warm water until soft. Squeeze the pulp to soften it, then strain the pulp to extract the juice. Discard the pulp.

3 In a heavy pan, roast half the grated coconut until it is brown and emits a nutty aroma. Using a mortar and pestle or food processor, grind the roasted coconut until it resembles sugar grains – this is called kerisik.

4 Heat the oil in a wok or earthenware pot, and stir in the rempah and cinnamon sticks until fragrant. Add the chicken strips. Pour in the coconut milk and tamarind water, and stir in the sugar. Reduce the heat and cook gently for about 10 minutes. Stir in half the ground roasted coconut to thicken the sauce and season.

5 In a bowl, mix the remaining grated coconut with the chillies, coriander and juice of 1 lime to serve as a relish. Cut the other lime into wedges. Spoon the chicken curry into a serving dish and garnish with a few coriander leaves. Serve with the coconut and chilli relish, the lime wedges to squeeze over it and a bowl of steamed rice.

COOK'S TIP
The palm sugar lends its unique sweet, caramelized flavour to the dish. If you cannot find palm sugar, you could try light muscovado (brown) sugar as a substitute.

Nutritional information per portion: Energy 487Kcal/2024kJ; Protein 29.2g; Carbohydrate 11.3g, of which sugars 10.6g; Fat 36.4g, of which saturates 19.2g; Cholesterol 150mg; Calcium 114mg; Fibre 4.4g; Sodium 267mg.

Jungle curry of guinea fowl

A traditional country curry from the north-central region of Thailand, this dish can be made with game, fish or chicken. Guinea fowl is not typical of Thai cuisine, but it works well in this curry.

SERVES 4

1 guinea fowl or similar game bird
15ml/1 tbsp vegetable oil
10ml/2 tsp green curry paste
15ml/1 tbsp Thai fish sauce
2.5cm/1in piece fresh galangal, peeled and finely chopped
15ml/1 tbsp fresh green peppercorns
3 kaffir lime leaves, torn
15ml/1 tbsp whisky, preferably Mekhong
300ml/½ pint/1¼ cups chicken stock
50g/2oz snake beans or yard-long beans, cut into 2.5cm/1in lengths (about ½ cup)
225g/8oz/3¼ cups chestnut mushrooms, sliced
1 piece drained canned bamboo shoot, about 50g/2oz, shredded
5ml/1 tsp dried chilli flakes, to garnish

1 Cut the guinea fowl into pieces, remove and discard the skin, then remove all the meat from the bones. Chop the meat into bitesize pieces and set aside while you make the sauce.

2 Heat the oil in a wok or frying pan and add the green curry paste. Stir-fry over a medium heat for about 30 seconds, until the paste gives off its aroma.

3 Add the fish sauce and the guinea fowl meat and stir-fry until the meat is browned all over. Add the galangal, peppercorns, lime leaves and whisky, then pour in the stock.

4 Bring to the boil. Add the vegetables, and cook gently for 2–3 minutes, until the guinea fowl is cooked through and the vegetables are tender. Spoon into a dish, sprinkle with chilli flakes, and serve.

Nutritional information per portion: Energy 321kcal/1345kJ; Protein 42.2g; Carbohydrate 1.1g, of which sugars 0.7g; Fat 15g, of which saturates 4.4g; Cholesterol 0mg; Calcium 73mg; Fibre 1.1g; Sodium 136mg.

Chinese duck curry

A richly spiced curry that shows Chinese influences on Thai cuisine. The duck is best marinated for as long as possible, although it still tastes good even if you only have time to marinate it briefly.

SERVES 4

4 duck breast portions, skin and
    bones removed, cut into bitesize pieces
30ml/2 tbsp five-spice powder
30ml/2 tbsp sesame oil
grated rind and juice of 1 orange
1 medium butternut squash, peeled
    and cubed
10ml/2 tsp Thai red curry paste
30ml/2 tbsp Thai fish sauce
15ml/1 tbsp palm sugar or light
    muscovado (brown) sugar
300ml/^{1}/$_2$ pint/1^1/$_4$ cups coconut milk
2 fresh red chillies, seeded
4 kaffir lime leaves, torn
small bunch coriander (cilantro),
    chopped, to garnish
fresh udon noodles, to serve

1 Place the duck meat in a bowl with the five-spice powder, sesame oil and orange rind and juice. Mix all the ingredients and coat the duck in the marinade. Cover the bowl with clear film (plastic wrap) and set aside in a cool place to marinate for 15 minutes.

2 Meanwhile, bring a pan of water to the boil. Add the squash and cook for 10–15 minutes, until just tender. Drain well and set aside.

3 Pour the marinade from the duck into a wok and heat until boiling.

4 Stir in the curry paste and cook for 2–3 minutes, until fragrant. Add the duck and cook for 3–4 minutes, stirring, until browned on all sides.

5 Add the fish sauce and palm sugar and cook for 2 minutes. Add the coconut milk and stir constantly until the mixture is smooth, then add the cooked squash, with the chillies and lime leaves.

6 Simmer, stirring often, for 5 minutes. Spoon into a dish, sprinkle with coriander and serve with udon noodles.

Nutritional information per portion: Energy 295kcal/1241kJ; Protein 31.4g; Carbohydrate 13.3g, of which sugars 12.3g; Fat 15.9g, of which saturates 3.1g; Cholesterol 165mg; Calcium 102mg; Fibre 2g; Sodium 427mg.

Lemon grass pork

Chillies and lemon grass flavour this simple stir-fry, while crunchy peanuts add an interesting contrast in texture. Look out for jars of chopped lemon grass, which are useful to have in reserve when the fresh herb is not readily available.

SERVES 4

675g/1½lb boneless pork loin
2 lemon grass stalks, finely chopped
4 spring onions (scallions), thinly sliced
5ml/1 tsp salt
12 black peppercorns, coarsely crushed
30ml/2 tbsp groundnut (peanut) oil
2 garlic cloves, chopped
2 fresh red chillies, seeded and chopped

5ml/1 tsp soft light brown sugar
30ml/2 tbsp Thai fish sauce
25g/1oz/¼ cup roasted unsalted
    peanuts, chopped
ground black pepper
coarsely torn coriander (cilantro) leaves,
    to garnish
cooked rice noodles, to serve

1 Trim any excess fat from the pork. Cut the meat across into 5mm/¼in thick slices, then cut each slice into 5mm/¼in strips. Put the pork into a bowl with the lemon grass, spring onions, salt and crushed peppercorns and mix well. Cover with clear film (plastic wrap) and leave to marinate in a cool place for 30 minutes.

2 Preheat a wok, add the oil and swirl it around. Add the pork mixture and stir-fry over a medium heat for about 3 minutes, until browned all over.

3 Add the garlic and red chillies and stir-fry for a further 5–8 minutes over a medium heat, until the pork is cooked through and tender.

4 Add the sugar, Thai fish sauce and chopped peanuts and toss to mix, then season to taste with freshly ground black pepper. Serve immediately on a bed of rice noodles, garnished with the coarsely torn coriander leaves.

Nutritional information per portion: Energy 205Kcal/856kJ; Protein 27.9g; Carbohydrate 4.8g, of which sugars 1.6g; Fat 9.5g, of which saturates 2.4g; Cholesterol 78mg; Calcium 1.8mg; Fibre 0.4g; Sodium 88mg.

Cambodian braised pork with ginger

This Cambodian curry is quick, tasty and beautifully warming thanks to the ginger and black pepper in the sauce. It is sure to be a popular choice for a family meal.

SERVES 4–6

1 litre/1¾ pints/4 cups pork stock or
    water
45ml/3 tbsp tuk trey (fish sauce)
30ml/2 tbsp soy sauce
15ml/1 tbsp sugar
4 garlic cloves, crushed
40g/1½oz fresh root ginger, peeled and
    finely shredded
15ml/1 tbsp ground black pepper
675g/1½lb pork shoulder or rump, fat
    trimmed, cut into bitesize cubes
steamed jasmine rice, crunchy salad and
    pickles or stir-fried greens, such as
    yard-long beans, to serve

1 In a large heavy pan, bring the pork stock or water, tuk trey and soy sauce to the boil.

2 Reduce the heat and add the sugar, garlic, ginger, black pepper and pork to the pan. Stir well.

3 Cover the pan and simmer for about 1½ hours, until the pork is tender and the liquid has reduced.

4 Serve the pork with rice and drizzle with the braising juices.

5 Accompany the dish with a fresh crunchy salad, pickled vegetables or stir-fried greens, such as the delicious stir-fried water spinach or yard-long beans, and a dipping sauce of nuoc cham, made with lime juice, fish sauce and garlic.

Nutritional information per portion: Energy 147Kcal/619kJ; Protein 24g; Carbohydrate 2.7g, of which sugars 2.7g; Fat 4g, of which saturates 2g; Cholesterol 71mg; Calcium 11mg; Fibre 0.1g; Sodium 81mg.

Chilli pork with curry leaves

Curry leaves and chillies are two of the hallmark ingredients used in the southern states of India. This recipe is from the state of Andhra Pradesh, where the hottest chillies are grown.

SERVES 4–6

30ml/2 tbsp vegetable oil

1 large onion, finely sliced

5cm/2in piece fresh root ginger, finely grated

4 garlic cloves, crushed

12 curry leaves

45ml/3 tbsp extra-hot curry paste, or 60ml/4 tbsp hot curry powder

15ml/1 tbsp chilli powder

5ml/1 tsp Chinese five-spice powder

5ml/1 tsp ground turmeric

900g/2lb pork, cubed

175ml/6fl oz/¾ cup thick coconut milk

salt

red onion, finely sliced, to garnish

Indian bread and fruit raita, to serve

1 Heat the oil in a karahi, wok or large pan, and fry the onion, ginger, garlic and curry leaves until the onion is soft.

2 Add the curry paste or powder, chilli and five-spice powder, turmeric and salt to the pan. Stir well.

3 Add the pork and stir well over a medium heat to seal and evenly brown the meat pieces. Keep stirring until the oil separates from the paste.

4 Cover the pan with the lid and cook for about 20–25 minutes. Stir in the coconut milk and simmer, still covered, for about 10 minutes or until the meat is cooked.

5 Toward the end of cooking, uncover the pan to allow the excess liquid to reduce and the sauce to thicken slightly. Garnish with red onion and serve with Indian bread, and with fruit raita, to provide a cooling effect.

Nutritional information per portion: Energy 283kcal/1182kJ; Protein 34.8g; Carbohydrate 11.1g, of which sugars 5.2g; Fat 11.5g, of which saturates 2.8g; Cholesterol 95mg; Calcium 58mg; Fibre 0.9g; Sodium 143mg.

Curried pork with pickled garlic

This very rich Thai-style curry is good with plain boiled rice and a light vegetable side dish, such as pak choi or curly kale.

SERVES 2

130g/4¹/₂oz lean pork steaks
30ml/2 tbsp vegetable oil
1 garlic clove, crushed
15ml/1 tbsp red curry paste
130ml/4¹/₂fl oz/generous ¹/₂ cup
    coconut cream
2.5cm/1in piece fresh root ginger,
    finely chopped
30ml/2 tbsp vegetable or chicken stock
30ml/2 tbsp Thai fish sauce
5ml/1 tsp sugar
2.5ml/¹/₂ tsp ground turmeric
10ml/2 tsp lemon juice
4 pickled garlic cloves, finely chopped
strips of lemon and lime rind, to garnish

1 Place the pork steaks in the freezer for 30–40 minutes, until firm, then, using a sharp knife, cut the meat into fine slivers, trimming off any excess fat.

2 Heat the oil in a wok or large, heavy frying pan and cook the garlic over low to medium heat until golden brown. Do not let it burn otherwise it will create a bitter taste. Add the curry paste and stir it in well.

3 Add the coconut cream and stir until the liquid begins to reduce and thicken. Stir in the pork. Cook for 2 minutes more, until the pork is cooked through. Add the ginger, stock, fish sauce, sugar and turmeric to the pan.

4 Stir constantly, then add the lemon juice and pickled garlic and heat through. Serve immediately in warmed bowls, garnished with strips of lemon and lime rind.

Nutritional information per portion: Energy 227kcal/947kJ; Protein 16.3g; Carbohydrate 9.8g, of which sugars 6.1g; Fat 14g, of which saturates 2.4g; Cholesterol 41mg; Calcium 30mg; Fibre 1g; Sodium 474mg.

Pork and pineapple coconut curry

This is a dish of contrasts: the pork is bathed in a creamy sauce spiked with hot curry paste, while the heat of chillies is balanced by the sweetness of the pineapple.

SERVES 4

400ml/14fl oz coconut milk

10ml/2 tsp Thai red curry paste

400g/14oz pork loin steaks, trimmed and thinly sliced

15ml/1 tbsp Thai fish sauce

5ml/1 tsp palm sugar (jaggery) or light muscovado (brown) sugar

15ml/1 tbsp tamarind juice, made by mixing tamarind paste with warm water

2 kaffir lime leaves, torn

1/2 medium pineapple, peeled and chopped

1 fresh red chilli, seeded and finely chopped and lime rind, to garnish

1 Pour the coconut milk into a bowl and let it settle, so that the cream rises to the surface. Scoop the cream into a measuring jug (cup). You should have about 250ml/8fl oz/1 cup. If necessary, add a little of the coconut milk. Pour the coconut cream into a large pan and bring it to the boil over high heat, stirring once or twice.

2 Cook the coconut cream for about 8 minutes, until the cream separates, stirring frequently to prevent it from sticking to the pan. Ladle a little coconut cream into a bowl and add the red curry paste.

3 Return the mixture to the pan and mix. Cook, stirring occasionally, for about 3 minutes, until the paste releases its fragrant aromas. Add the pork, fish sauce, sugar and tamarind juice. Cook, stirring, for 2–3 minutes, until the sugar has dissolved and the pork is no longer pink.

4 Add the remaining coconut milk and the lime leaves. Bring to the boil, then add the pineapple pieces. Reduce the heat and simmer for about 3 minutes, or until the pork is cooked. Spoon into a serving bowl or four individual bowls and sprinkle with the chilli and lime rind. Serve.

Nutritional information per portion: Energy 187kcal/790kJ; Protein 22.2g; Carbohydrate 15.3g, of which sugars 15.3g; Fat 4.5g, of which saturates 1.6g; Cholesterol 63mg; Calcium 55mg; Fibre 1.2g; Sodium 449mg.

Malay lamb korma with coconut milk

Adapted from the traditional Indian korma, the creamy Malay version is flavoured with coconut milk. This tasty curry is often accompanied by a fragrant rice or flatbread and a salad or sambal.

SERVES 4–6

25g/1oz fresh root ginger, peeled
   and chopped
4 garlic cloves, chopped
2 red chillies, seeded and chopped
10ml/2 tsp garam masala
10ml/2 tsp ground coriander
5ml/1 tsp ground cumin
5ml/1 tsp ground turmeric
675g/1¹/₂lb lamb shoulder, cut into
   bitesize cubes
45ml/3 tbsp ghee, or 30ml/2 tbsp vegetable
   oil and 15g/¹/₂oz/1 tbsp butter

2 onions, halved lengthways and sliced along
   the grain
2.5ml/¹/₂ tsp sugar
4–6 cardamom pods, bruised
1 cinnamon stick
400ml/14fl oz/1²/₃ cups coconut milk
salt and ground black pepper
30ml/2 tbsp roasted peanuts, crushed, and
   fresh coriander (cilantro) and mint leaves,
   coarsely chopped, to garnish

1 Using a mortar and pestle or food processor, grind the ginger, garlic and chillies to a paste. Stir in the garam masala, ground coriander, cumin and turmeric. Put the lamb into a shallow dish and rub the paste into it. Cover and leave to marinate for 1 hour.

2 Heat the ghee or oil and butter in a heavy pan or flameproof pot. Add the onions and sugar, and cook until brown and almost caramelized. Stir in the cardamom pods and cinnamon stick and add the lamb with the marinade. Mix well and cook until the meat is browned all over.

3 Pour in the coconut milk, stir well and bring to the boil. Reduce the heat, cover the pan and cook the meat gently for 30–40 minutes until tender. Make sure the meat doesn't become dry and stir in a little extra coconut milk, or water, if necessary.

4 Season to taste with salt and pepper. Sprinkle the peanuts over and garnish with the coriander and mint. Serve immediately.

Nutritional information per portion: Energy 267kcal/1117kJ; Protein 24.3g; Carbohydrate 8.5g, of which sugars 6.8g; Fat 15.4g, of which saturates 6.4g; Cholesterol 86mg; Calcium 46mg; Fibre 1.2g; Sodium 211mg.

Fragrant lamb curry

Essentially a popular Muslim lamb dish known as rezala, this curry comes from Bengal. Rose water is typically added to enhance the flavour, and saffron adds a delicate yellow colour.

SERVES 4

1 large onion, roughly chopped

10ml/2 tsp grated fresh root ginger

10ml/2 tsp crushed garlic

4–5 cloves

2.5ml/^{1}/$_2$ tsp black peppercorns

6 green cardamom pods

5cm/2in cinnamon stick, halved

8 lamb rib chops

60ml/4 tbsp vegetable oil

1 large onion, finely sliced

175ml/6fl oz/^{3}/$_4$ cup natural (plain) yogurt

50g/2oz/^{1}/$_4$ cup butter

5ml/1 tsp salt

2.5ml/^{1}/$_2$ tsp ground cumin

2.5ml/^{1}/$_2$ tsp hot chilli powder

2.5ml/^{1}/$_2$ tsp freshly grated nutmeg

2.5ml/^{1}/$_2$ tsp sugar

15ml/1 tbsp lime juice

pinch of saffron, steeped in 15ml/1 tbsp hot
    water for 10–15 minutes

15ml/1 tbsp rose water

rose petals or other flower petals, to garnish

1 Process the onion in a blender or food processor. Add a little water if necessary to form a purée. Put the purée in a glass bowl and add the ginger, garlic, cloves, peppercorns, cardamom pods, and cinnamon. Mix well.

2 Put the lamb in a glass dish and add the spice mixture. Mix thoroughly, cover and leave to marinate for 3–4 hours.

3 In a wok, karahi or large pan, heat the oil over a medium-high heat and fry the sliced onion for 6–7 minutes, until golden brown. Remove the onion slices, squeezing out as much oil as possible back into the pan. Drain the onion on kitchen paper. In the remaining oil, fry the lamb chops for 5 minutes, stirring frequently. Reduce the heat, cover and simmer for 5–7 minutes.

4 Meanwhile, mix the yogurt and butter together in a pan and cook over a low heat for 5 minutes, then stir into the lamb chops along with the salt. Add the cumin and chilli powder and cover the pan. Cook for 45–50 minutes until the chops are tender.

5 Add the nutmeg and sugar, cook for 1–2 minutes and add the lime juice, saffron and rose water. Stir well and simmer for 2 minutes. Serve garnished with the fried onion and rose petals.

Nutritional information per portion: Energy 399kcal/1664kJ; Protein 22.6g; Carbohydrate 35.1g, of which sugars 7.5g; Fat 18.8g, of which saturates 7.8g; Cholesterol 74mg; Calcium 70mg; Fibre 1.4g; Sodium 131mg.

Lahore-style lamb

Named after the city of Lahore in Pakistan, this hearty curry has a wonderfully aromatic flavour imparted by warm spices such as cloves, black peppercorns and cinnamon.

SERVES 4

60ml/4 tbsp vegetable oil
1 bay leaf
2 cloves
4 black peppercorns
1 onion, sliced
450g/1lb lean lamb, boned and cubed
1.5ml/¼ tsp ground turmeric
7.5ml/1½ tsp chilli powder
5ml/1 tsp crushed coriander seeds
2.5cm/1in piece cinnamon stick
5ml/1 tsp crushed garlic
7.5ml/1½ tsp salt
1.5 litres/2½ pints/6¼ cups water
50g/2oz/⅓ cup chana dhal (yellow lentils) or yellow split peas
2 tomatoes, quartered
2 fresh green chillies, chopped
15ml/1 tbsp chopped fresh coriander (cilantro)

1 Heat the oil in a wok, karahi or large pan. Lower the heat slightly and add the bay leaf, cloves, peppercorns and onion. Fry for about 5 minutes, or until the onion is golden brown.

2 Add the cubed lamb, turmeric, chilli powder, coriander seeds, cinnamon stick, garlic and most of the salt, and stir-fry for about 5 minutes over a medium heat.

3 Pour in 900ml/1½ pints/3¾ cups of the water and cover the pan. Bring to the boil, then simmer for 35–40 minutes or until the lamb is tender.

4 Put the chana dhal or split peas into a large pan with the remaining water and a good pinch of salt. Boil for 12–15 minutes, or until the water has almost evaporated and the lentils or peas are soft. If it is too thick, add a little extra water.

5 When the lamb is tender, remove the lid or foil and stir-fry the mixture using a wooden spoon, until some free oil begins to appear on the sides of the pan.

6 Add the cooked lentils to the lamb and mix together. Stir in the tomatoes, chillies and fresh coriander and serve.

Nutritional information per portion: Energy 331kcal/1379kJ; Protein 26.5g; Carbohydrate 9.7g, of which sugars 1.9g; Fat 20.6g, of which saturates 5.6g; Cholesterol 83mg; Calcium 40mg; Fibre 1.8g; Sodium 99mg.

Spiced lamb with tomatoes

Select lean tender lamb from the leg for this lightly spiced curry with succulent peppers and wedges of onion. Serve with warm naan bread.

SERVES 6

1.5kg/3¼lb lean boneless lamb, cubed
250ml/8fl oz/1 cup natural (plain) yogurt
30ml/2 tbsp sunflower oil
3 onions
2 red (bell) peppers, cut into chunks
3 garlic cloves, finely chopped
1 red chilli, seeded and chopped
2.5cm/1in piece fresh root ginger, peeled
     and chopped
30ml/2 tbsp mild curry paste
2 x 400g/14oz cans chopped tomatoes
large pinch of saffron strands, ground
     to powder
800g/1¾lb plum tomatoes, halved,
     seeded and cut into chunks
salt and ground black pepper
chopped fresh coriander (cilantro),
     to garnish

1 Mix the lamb with the yogurt in a bowl. Cover and chill for about 1 hour. Heat the oil in a wok or large pan. Drain the lamb and reserve the yogurt, then cook the lamb in batches until it is golden on all sides – this takes about 15 minutes. Remove from the pan and set aside.

2 Cut two of the onions into wedges and add to the oil remaining in the pan. Fry the onion wedges over a medium heat for about 10 minutes, or until they begin to colour. Add the peppers and cook for 5 minutes. Remove the vegetables from the pan and set aside.

3 Meanwhile, chop the remaining onion. Add it to the oil remaining in the pan with the garlic, chilli and ginger, and cook, stirring often, until softened. Stir in the curry paste and canned tomatoes with the reserved yogurt marinade. Replace the lamb, season to taste and stir well. Bring to the boil, reduce the heat and simmer for about 30 minutes.

4 Dissolve the ground saffron in a little boiling water then add to the curry. Replace the onion and pepper mixture. Add the fresh tomatoes, then simmer for 15 minutes. Garnish with coriander to serve.

Nutritional information per portion: Energy 559kcal/2343kJ; Protein 54.4g; Carbohydrate 20.5g, of which sugars 18.8g; Fat 29.6g, of which saturates 13.5g; Cholesterol 191mg; Calcium 139mg; Fibre 4.6g; Sodium 278mg.

Lamb and new potato curry

This dish makes the most of an economical cut of meat by cooking it slowly until the meat is falling from the bone. Chillies and coconut cream add lots of flavour.

SERVES 4

25g/1oz/2 tbsp butter
2 onions, sliced into rings
4 garlic cloves, crushed
2.5ml/¹/₂ tsp ground cumin
2.5ml/¹/₂ tsp ground coriander
2.5ml/¹/₂ tsp turmeric
2.5ml/¹/₂ tsp cayenne pepper
2–3 red chillies, seeded and chopped
300ml/¹/₂ pint/1¹/₄ cups chicken stock
200ml/7fl oz/scant 1 cup coconut cream
4 lamb shanks, excess fat removed
450g/1lb new potatoes, halved
6 ripe tomatoes, quartered
salt and ground black pepper
fresh coriander (cilantro) leaves,
    to garnish
spicy rice, to serve

1 Preheat the oven to 160°C/325°F/Gas 3. Melt the butter in a large flameproof casserole, add the onions and cook, stirring frequently, over a low heat for 6–8 minutes, until beginning to soften. Add the garlic and fry for 3–4 minutes. Stir in the spices and chillies, then cook for a further 2 minutes.

2 Stir in the hot chicken stock and coconut cream. Place the lamb shanks in the liquid and cover the casserole with foil. Cook in the oven for about 2 hours, turning the shanks twice in the cooking liquid, first after about 1 hour of cooking and again roughly another 30 minutes later.

3 Par-boil the potatoes for about 10 minutes or until barely tender, drain and add to the casserole with the tomatoes, then cook uncovered in the oven for a further 35 minutes. Season to taste with salt and pepper. Serve garnished with coriander leaves and accompanied by the spicy rice.

Nutritional information per portion: Energy 364kcal/1528kJ; Protein 23.5g; Carbohydrate 30.5g, of which sugars 12.1g; Fat 17.4g, of which saturates 8.8g; Cholesterol 89mg; Calcium 58mg; Fibre 3.5g; Sodium 205mg.

Lamb dhansak

This piquant curry features lamb flavoured with a medley of spices, seeds and herbs in a fragrant sauce made from lentils and aubergines.

SERVES 4

45ml/3 tbsp sunflower oil

1 large onion, finely chopped

10ml/2 tsp each ginger and garlic purée

5ml/1 tsp coriander seeds

2.5ml/1/2 tsp cumin seeds

4 green cardamom pods

2.5cm/1in cinnamon stick, broken

10–12 black peppercorns

2 bay leaves

5–6 fenugreek seeds

2.5ml/1/2 tsp black mustard seeds

5ml/1 tsp chilli powder or to taste

675g/11/2lb boned leg of lamb, cubed

150g/5oz canned tomatoes

75g/3oz/1/3 cup each yellow split peas
    and red split lentils

30ml/2 tbsp sunflower oil

1 medium onion, finely chopped

2 green chillies, chopped

5ml/1 tsp ground turmeric

1 small aubergine (eggplant), cubed

5ml/1 tsp salt or to taste

30ml/2 tbsp lime juice

30ml/2 tbsp chopped coriander (cilantro)

1 In a heavy pan, heat the oil and fry the onion until soft, then add the ginger and garlic purées and fry until brown. Grind the coriander, cumin, cardamom, cinnamon, peppercorns, bay leaves, fenugreek and mustard seeds finely in a food processor. Add the chilli and ground spices to the onion and cook for 2 minutes.

2 Add the meat and fry over a high heat until brown. Add the tomatoes and salt, and pour in 120ml/4fl oz/1/2 cup warm water. Bring the pan to the boil, cover and simmer for 35–40 minutes.

3 Wash the split peas and lentils and drain. Heat the oil in a medium pan and fry the onion and chillies until browned, about 8–9 minutes. Stir in the turmeric, split peas, lentils and aubergine.

4 Pour in 600ml/1 pint/21/2 cups warm water, and simmer for 20–25 minutes, stirring. Add salt, then push the lentils through a sieve (strainer). Discard any coarse mixture left in the sieve.

5 Add the lime juice to the lentils. Pour over the lamb and simmer for 20 minutes, stirring occasionally. Stir in half of the coriander and remove from the heat. Serve garnished with the remaining coriander.

Nutritional information per portion: Energy 470kcal/1970kJ; Protein 32.7g; Carbohydrate 36.5g, of which sugars 9g; Fat 22.7g, of which saturates 7.1g; Cholesterol 85.5mg; Calcium 106mg; Fibre 4.8g; Sodium 133mg.

Javanese goat curry

This slow-cooked curry boasts a host of spices, flavourings and nuts. It originates in Java where goat's meat is commonly used, although lamb could be used instead.

SERVES 4

30–60ml/2–4 tbsp coconut oil

10ml/2 tsp shrimp paste

15ml/1 tbsp palm sugar (jaggery)

5ml/1 tsp coriander seeds

5ml/1 tsp cumin seeds

2.5ml/$\frac{1}{2}$ tsp grated nutmeg

2.5ml/$\frac{1}{2}$ tsp ground black pepper

2–3 lemon grass stalks, halved

700g/1lb 9oz boneless shoulder or leg of goat, or lamb, cut into bitesize pieces

400g/14oz can coconut milk

200ml/7fl oz/scant 1 cup water

12 yard-long beans

1 bunch fresh coriander (cilantro) leaves, roughly chopped

FOR THE SPICE PASTE

2–3 each shallots, garlic cloves and chillies, chopped

25g/1oz galangal, chopped

10ml/2 tsp ground turmeric

1 lemon grass stalk, chopped

2–3 macadamia nuts, ground

1 For the spice paste, grind all the ingredients in a food processor or blender, or crush to a paste with a pestle and mortar.

2 Heat 15–30ml/1–2 tbsp of the oil in a heavy pan, stir in the spice paste and fry for 2 minutes. Add the shrimp paste and palm sugar and continue to stir-fry for 1–2 minutes.

3 Heat the remaining 15–30ml/1–2 tbsp oil in a large, flameproof casserole. Stir in the coriander seeds, cumin seeds, nutmeg and black pepper.

4 Add the spice paste and lemon grass. Stir-fry for 2–3 minutes, until the mixture is fragrant.

5 Add the meat, coconut milk and water to the pan and stir well to mix. Bring to the boil, then reduce the heat, cover and simmer for 3 hours.

6 Add the beans and cook for 10–15 minutes.Toss some of the coriander leaves into the curry and season to taste. Garnish with the remaining coriander and serve with rice and chillies.

Nutritional information per portion: Energy 450kcal/1877kJ; Protein 37.9g; Carbohydrate 10.8g, of which sugars 9.1g; Fat 28.7g, of which saturates 10.3g; Cholesterol 146mg; Calcium 129mg; Fibre 2.4g; Sodium 375mg.

Mussaman beef

This dish is traditionally based on beef, but chicken, lamb or tofu can be used instead. Mussaman curry paste, available from specialist Asian stores, imparts a rich, sweet and spicy flavour.

SERVES 4–6

675g/1¹⁄₂lb stewing steak
600ml/1 pint/2¹⁄₂ cups coconut milk
250ml/8fl oz/1 cup coconut cream
45ml/3 tbsp Mussaman curry paste
30ml/2 tbsp Thai fish sauce
15ml/1 tbsp palm sugar (jaggery) or light
** muscovado (brown) sugar**
60ml/4 tbsp tamarind juice (tamarind
** paste mixed with warm water)**
6 green cardamom pods
1 cinnamon stick
1 large potato, about 225g/8oz, cut into
** even chunks**
1 onion, cut into wedges
50g/2oz/¹⁄₂ cup roasted peanuts

1 Trim off any excess fat from the stewing steak, then, using a sharp knife, cut it into 2.5cm/1in chunks. Pour the coconut milk into a large, heavy pan and bring to the boil over a medium heat. Add the chunks of beef to the coconut milk, reduce the heat to low, partially cover the pan and simmer gently for about 40–45 minutes, or until tender.

2 Pour the coconut cream into a separate pan. Cook over a medium heat, stirring constantly, for about 5 minutes, or until it separates. Stir in the Mussaman curry paste and cook rapidly for 2–3 minutes, until fragrant and thoroughly blended.

3 Add the coconut cream and curry paste mixture to the pan with the beef and stir until thoroughly blended. Simmer for a further 4–5 minutes, stirring occasionally.

4 Add the fish sauce, sugar, tamarind juice, cardamom pods, cinnamon stick, potato chunks and onion wedges. Continue to simmer for a further 15–20 minutes, or until the potato is cooked and tender.

5 Add most of the roasted peanuts to the pan and stir well. Cook for 5 minutes, then transfer to warmed bowls, garnish with the reserved peanuts and serve immediately.

Nutritional information per portion: Energy 626kcal/2610kJ; Protein 44.6g; Carbohydrate 24.8g, of which sugars 15.4g; Fat 39.3g, of which saturates 22.7g; Cholesterol 98mg; Calcium 74mg; Fibre 1.6g; Sodium 288mg.

Beef rendang

This spicy dish is slowly simmered on top of the stove and is usually served without much liquid and the meat quite dry. If you prefer more sauce, add a little more water.

SERVES 6–8

2 onions or 5–6 shallots, chopped
4 garlic cloves, chopped
2.5cm/1in piece each fresh galangal and
    root ginger, peeled and sliced
4–6 fresh red chillies, seeded and chopped
lower part of 1 lemon grass stalk, sliced
5ml/1 tsp ground turmeric
1kg/2¼lb prime beef, in one piece
5ml/1 tsp coriander seeds, dry-fried
5ml/1 tsp cumin seeds, dry-fried
2 kaffir lime leaves, torn into small pieces
2 x 400ml/14fl oz cans coconut milk
300ml/½ pint/1¼ cups water
30ml/2 tbsp dark soy sauce
5ml/1 tsp tamarind pulp, soaked in
    60ml/4 tbsp warm water
8–10 small new potatoes, scrubbed
salt and ground black pepper
deep-fried onions, sliced fresh red chillies
    and spring onions (scallions), to garnish

1 Put the onions or shallots in a food processor. Add the garlic, galangal, ginger, chillies, sliced lemon grass and turmeric. Process to a fine paste or grind using a pestle and mortar.

2 Cut the meat into cubes using a large, sharp knife, then place the cubes in a bowl. Grind the dry-fried coriander and cumin seeds, then add to the meat with the onion and chilli paste and kaffir lime leaves; stir well. Cover and leave in a cool place to marinate for 1 hour.

3 Pour the coconut milk and water into a wok or large pan, then stir in the spiced meat and the soy sauce. Strain the tamarind water and add to the wok or pan. Stir over a medium heat until the liquid boils, then simmer gently, half-covered with a lid, for about 1½ hours.

4 Add the potatoes to the pan and simmer for 20–25 minutes, or until the meat and potatoes are tender. Season and serve, garnished with deep-fried onions, chillies and spring onions.

Nutritional information per portion: Energy 289kcal/1210kJ; Protein 30.2g; Carbohydrate 15.4g, of which sugars 8.6g; Fat 12.2g, of which saturates 5g; Cholesterol 73mg; Calcium 63mg; Fibre 1.4g; Sodium 465mg.

Madras beef curry

Although Madras is renowned for the best vegetarian food in India, meat-based recipes such as this beef curry are also popular. This recipe is from the area's small Muslim community.

SERVES 4–6

60ml/4 tbsp vegetable oil
1 large onion, finely sliced
3–4 cloves
4 green cardamoms
2 whole star anise
4 fresh green chillies, chopped
2 fresh or dried red chillies, chopped
45ml/3 tbsp Madras masala paste
5ml/1 tsp ground turmeric
450g/1lb lean beef, cubed
60ml/4 tbsp tamarind juice
sugar, to taste
salt
a few fresh coriander (cilantro) leaves,
    chopped, to garnish
pilau rice and mixed salad, to serve

1 Heat the vegetable oil in a wok, karahi or large pan over a medium heat. Add the onion slices and fry for 8–9 minutes, stirring occasionally, until they soften and turn golden brown.

2 Lower the heat, add all the spice ingredients to the pan, and fry for a further 2–3 minutes, stirring constantly, until the spices release their fragrances.

3 Add the beef to the pan and mix well. Cover and cook over a low heat until the beef is cooked through and tender. Cook uncovered on a high heat for the last few minutes to reduce and produce a thicker sauce.

4 Fold in the tamarind juice, sugar and salt. Reheat the dish and garnish with the chopped coriander leaves. Serve with pilau rice and a simple mixed salad.

Nutritional information per portion: Energy 524kcal/2180kJ; Protein 37.6g; Carbohydrate 13.8g, of which sugars 7.4g; Fat 36g, of which saturates 13.8g; Cholesterol 133mg; Calcium 65mg; Fibre 2.6g; Sodium 160mg.

Oxtail in hot tangy sauce

Considered a delicacy in some parts of South-east Asia, oxtail and the tails of water buffalo are cooked for special feasts and celebrations. It is served with steamed rice, or fresh, crusty bread.

SERVES 4–6

8 shallots, chopped

8 garlic cloves, chopped

4–6 fresh red chillies, seeded and chopped

25g/1oz fresh galangal, chopped

30ml/2 tbsp rice flour or plain (all-purpose) flour

15ml/1 tbsp ground turmeric

8–12 oxtail joints, cut roughly the same size and trimmed of fat

45ml/3 tbsp vegetable oil

225g/8oz tamarind pulp

400g/14oz can plum tomatoes, drained and chopped

2 lemon grass stalks, halved and bruised

a handful of fresh kaffir lime leaves

30–45ml/2–3 tbsp sugar

salt and ground black pepper

fresh coriander (cilantro) leaves, roughly chopped

1 Using a food processor, grind the shallots, garlic, chillies and galangal to a coarse paste. Mix the flour with the ground turmeric and spread it on a flat surface. Roll the oxtail in the flour and set aside.

2 Heat the oil in a heavy pan or flameproof pot. Stir in the spice paste and cook until fragrant. Add the oxtail and brown on all sides.

3 Soak the tamarind pulp in 600ml/1 pint/2½ cups water, squeeze it, strain the juice and discard the pulp and seeds.

4 Add the tomatoes, lemon grass stalks, lime leaves and tamarind juice to the oxtail. Pour in enough water to cover the oxtail, and bring it to the boil. Skim off any fat from the surface. Reduce the heat, cover the pan with a lid and simmer the oxtail for 2 hours.

5 Stir in the sugar, season with salt and pepper and continue to cook, uncovered, for a further 30–40 minutes, until the meat is very tender. Sprinkle with the coriander and serve the curry immediately, straight from the pan.

Nutritional information per portion: Energy 386kcal/1611kJ; Protein 34.5g; Carbohydrate 11.3g, of which sugars 6.6g; Fat 22.6g, of which saturates 7.7g; Cholesterol 125mg; Calcium 31mg; Fibre 1.2g; Sodium 191mg.

Green beef curry with Thai aubergines

This is quick to cook, so it is essential that you use good-quality meat. Sirloin is recommended here, but tender rump or even fillet steak could be used instead, if they are available.

SERVES 4–6

15ml/1 tbsp vegetable oil

45ml/3 tbsp Thai green curry paste

600ml/1 pint/2½ cups coconut milk

450g/1lb beef sirloin, trimmed of excess
   fat, chilled and sliced into thin strips

4 kaffir lime leaves, torn

15–30ml/1–2 tbsp Thai fish sauce

5ml/1 tsp palm sugar (jaggery) or light
   muscovado (brown) sugar

150g/5oz small Thai aubergines
   (eggplants), halved

a small handful of fresh Thai basil,
   roughly chopped

2 fresh green chillies, seeded and finely
   shredded plus extra Thai basil sprigs,
   to garnish

1 Heat the oil in a large, heavy pan or wok. Add the curry paste and cook for 1–2 minutes.

2 Stir in half the coconut milk, a little at a time. Cook, stirring frequently, for about 5–6 minutes, until an oily sheen appears on the surface.

3 Add the beef to the pan with the kaffir lime leaves, fish sauce, sugar and aubergine.

4 Cook for 2–3 minutes, then add the remaining coconut milk.

5 Bring back to a simmer and cook until the meat and aubergines are tender. Stir in the Thai basil.

6 Spoon the curry into a heated dish or on to warmed individual plates. Sprinkle the finely shredded chillies over the top of the curry, add the sprigs of basil and serve immediately.

Nutritional information per portion: Energy 147kcal/619kJ; Protein 18.2g; Carbohydrate 6.4g, of which sugars 6.3g; Fat 5.6g, of which saturates 1.9g; Cholesterol 38mg; Calcium 36mg; Fibre 0.5g; Sodium 341mg.

Beef curry in sweet peanut sauce

This curry is deliciously rich and thick. It is usually served with rice, but would also make a good filling for pitta breads, or it could be eaten with chapatis.

SERVES 4–6

600ml/1 pint/2½ cups coconut milk

45ml/3 tbsp red curry paste

45ml/3 tbsp fish sauce

30ml/2 tbsp light muscovado
(brown) sugar

2 lemon grass stalks, bruised

450g/1lb rump (round) steak, cut into
thin strips

75g/3oz/¾ cup roasted peanuts, ground

2 fresh red chillies, sliced

5 kaffir lime leaves, torn

salt and ground black pepper

2 salted eggs, cut in wedges, and 10–15
Thai basil leaves, to garnish

1 Pour half the coconut milk into a large, heavy pan or wok. Place over a medium heat and bring slowly to the boil, stirring constantly until the milk separates.

2 Stir the red curry paste into the coconut milk and cook for 2–3 minutes until the mixture is fragrant and thoroughly blended. Add the fish sauce, sugar and bruised lemon grass stalks. Mix well until combined.

3 Continue to cook until the colour deepens. Gradually add the remaining coconut milk, stirring constantly. Bring back to the boil, stirring constantly.

4 Add the beef and peanuts. Cook, stirring constantly, for 8–10 minutes, or until most of the liquid has evaporated. Add the chillies and lime leaves. Season to taste and serve, garnished with wedges of salted eggs and Thai basil leaves.

Nutritional information per portion: Energy 227kcal/953kJ; Protein 21g; Carbohydrate 14.3g, of which sugars 11.5g; Fat 9.9g, of which saturates 2.6g; Cholesterol 44mg; Calcium 92mg; Fibre 2.5g; Sodium 723mg.

Dry beef and peanut butter curry

Although this is called a dry curry, the method of cooking, with ingredients such as coconut milk and peanut butter, helps to keep the beef tender and succulent.

SERVES 4–6

400g/14oz can coconut milk
900g/2lb stewing beef, finely chopped
300ml/1/2 pint/1¼ cups beef stock
30–45ml/2–3 tbsp red curry paste
30ml/2 tbsp crunchy peanut butter
juice of 2 limes
lime slices, shredded coriander (cilantro)
 and fresh red chilli slices, to garnish
jasmine rice, to serve

1 Strain the coconut milk into a bowl, retaining the thicker coconut milk in the sieve (strainer).

2 Pour the thin coconut milk from the bowl into a large, heavy pan or wok, then scrape in half the residue from the sieve. Reserve the remaining thick coconut milk. Add the chopped beef to the pan. Pour in the beef stock and bring the mixture to the boil. Reduce the heat, cover the pan and simmer gently for about 50 minutes.

3 Strain the beef, reserving the cooking liquid, and place a cupful of this liquid in a wok. Stir in 30–45ml/2–3 tbsp of the curry paste, according to taste. Boil rapidly until all the liquid has evaporated. Stir in the reserved thick coconut milk, the peanut butter and the beef. Simmer, uncovered, for 15–20 minutes, adding a little more cooking liquid if the mixture starts to stick to the pan, but keep the curry dry.

4 Just before serving, stir in the lime juice. Serve with jasmine rice, garnished with the lime slices, shredded coriander and sliced red chillies.

Nutritional information per portion: Energy 296kcal/1238kJ; Protein 35.2g; Carbohydrate 4.9g, of which sugars 4.5g; Fat 15.2g, of which saturates 4.8g; Cholesterol 103mg; Calcium 66mg; Fibre 0.7g; Sodium 262mg.

Slow-cooked buffalo in coconut milk

Cook this slowly for tender meat and a rich sauce. Buffalo has little fat so lends itself to long, gentle cooking, otherwise it is similar in taste and structure to beef.

SERVES 6

1kg/2¼lb buffalo or beef, cubed
115g/4oz fresh coconut, grated
45ml/3 tbsp coconut oil
2 onions, sliced
3 lemon grass stalks, halved
2 cinnamon sticks
3–4 lime leaves
1.2 litres/2 pints/5 cups coconut milk
15ml/1 tbsp tamarind paste dissolved in
     90ml/6 tbsp water
15ml/1 tbsp sugar
salt and ground black pepper

15ml/1 tbsp vegetable oil, 6 shallots, carrot
     strips, cooked rice and a salad, to serve

FOR THE SPICE PASTE
8 red chillies, seeded and chopped
8 shallots, chopped
4–6 garlic cloves, chopped
50g/2oz galangal, chopped
25g/1oz fresh turmeric, chopped
15ml/1 tbsp coriander seeds
10ml/2 tsp cumin seeds
5ml/1 tsp black peppercorns

1 First make the spice paste. Grind the chillies, shallots, garlic, galangal and turmeric to a smooth paste. In a frying pan, dry-fry the coriander, cumin and peppercorns for 2–3 minutes. Grind the dry-fried spices to a powder then stir into the spice paste.

2 Put the buffalo or beef in a large bowl and mix in the spice paste. Leave to marinate for at least 2 hours. Dry-fry the coconut in a heavy pan until brown. Grind the coconut in a food processor. Set aside.

3 Heat the oil in a flameproof casserole. Add the onions, lemon grass, cinnamon and lime leaves, and fry for 5 minutes. Add the beef and paste and fry until browned. Add the coconut milk and tamarind juice and bring to the boil. Reduce the heat and simmer gently for 2–4 hours for beef (4 hours for buffalo).

4 Stir in the sugar and ground coconut, cover and cook for 4 hours if using buffalo and 2–4 hours if using beef, stirring occasionally, until the meat is tender and the sauce is very thick. Season. Fry the shallots in the oil. Spoon the meat on to a serving dish, garnish with the shallots and carrots and serve with rice and a salad.

Nutritional information per portion: Energy 494kcal/2064kJ; Protein 40.6g; Carbohydrate 20.9g, of which sugars 18.8g; Fat 28.2g, of which saturates 17g; Cholesterol 97mg; Calcium 95mg; Fibre 3.9g; Sodium 335mg.

Spiced pumpkin wedges and sautéed spinach

Warmly spiced roasted pumpkin, combined with creamy spinach and the fire of chilli, makes a lovely accompaniment for curries, grills and roasts.

SERVES 4–6

10ml/2 tsp coriander seeds
5ml/1 tsp each cumin and fennel seeds
5–10ml/1–2 tsp cinnamon
2 dried red chillies, chopped
coarse salt
2 garlic cloves
30ml/2 tbsp olive oil
1 pumpkin, halved, seeded, cut into wedges

FOR THE SAUTÉED SPINACH
30–45ml/2–3 tbsp pine nuts
30–45ml/2–3 tbsp olive oil
1 red onion, halved and sliced
1–2 dried red chillies, finely sliced
1 apple, peeled, cored and sliced
2 garlic cloves, crushed
5–10ml/1–2 tsp ground roasted cumin
10ml/2 tsp clear honey
450g/1lb spinach, steamed and chopped
60–75ml/4–5 tbsp double (heavy) cream
fresh spinach leaves, to garnish

1 Preheat the oven to 200°C/400°F/Gas 6. Grind the coriander, cumin and fennel seeds, cinnamon and chillies with a little coarse salt in a mortar with a pestle. Add the garlic and a little of the olive oil and pound to form a paste. Rub the spice mixture over the pumpkin segments and place them, skin side down, in an ovenproof dish or roasting pan. Bake the spiced pumpkin for 35–40 minutes, or until tender.

2 To make the spinach, roast the pine nuts in a dry frying pan until golden, then transfer to a plate. Add the olive oil to the pan. Sauté the onion with the chilli until soft, then stir in the apple and garlic. Once the apple begins to colour, stir in most of the pine nuts, most of the cumin and the honey.

3 Toss in the spinach and, once it has heated through, stir in most of the cream. Season to taste and remove from the heat. Swirl the last of the cream on top, sprinkle with the reserved pine nuts and roasted cumin, and spinach leaves. Serve hot.

Nutritional information per portion: Energy 456kcal/1897kJ; Protein 18.9g; Carbohydrate 22.1g, of which sugars 17.1g; Fat 31.9g, of which saturates 13.2g; Cholesterol 45mg; Calcium 635mg; Fibre 10g; Sodium 337mg.

Spiced coconut mushrooms

Here is a simple and delicious way to cook mushrooms. They can be served with almost any Indian meal as well as with traditional grilled or roasted meats and poultry.

SERVES 4

30ml/2 tbsp groundnut (peanut) oil
2 garlic cloves, finely chopped
2 fresh red chillies, seeded and sliced
    into rings
3 shallots or 1 small onion, finely
    chopped
225g/8oz/3 cups brown cap (cremini)
    mushrooms, thickly sliced
150ml/¼ pint/⅔ cup coconut milk
30ml/2 tbsp chopped fresh
    coriander (cilantro)
salt and ground black pepper

1 Heat a karahi, wok or heavy frying pan until hot, add the groundnut oil and swirl it around. Add the garlic and chillies, then stir-fry for a few seconds.

2 Add the chopped shallots or onion and cook them for about 2–3 minutes, stirring constantly, until softened. Add the mushrooms and stir-fry for about 3 minutes.

3 Pour the coconut milk into the pan and bring to the boil. Boil rapidly over high heat until the liquid has reduced by about half and has thickened to coat the mushrooms. Season to taste with salt and black pepper.

4 Sprinkle over the chopped fresh coriander and toss the mushrooms gently to mix. Serve immediately.

Nutritional information per portion: Energy 76kcal/313kJ; Protein 2g; Carbohydrate 3.4g, of which sugars 3g; Fat 6.1g, of which saturates 0.8g; Cholesterol 0mg; Calcium 26mg; Fibre 0.8g; Sodium 46mg.

Okra and tomato tagine

This spicy vegetable stew is a North African speciality and similar dishes exist throughout the Middle East. Although simply spiced, the curry has a deliciously piquant flavour.

SERVES 4

350g/12oz okra
5–6 tomatoes
2 small onions
2 garlic cloves, crushed
1 fresh green chilli, seeded and
    roughly chopped
5ml/1 tsp paprika
small handful of fresh
    coriander (cilantro)
30ml/2 tbsp sunflower oil
juice of 1 lemon

1 Trim the okra and then cut it into 1cm/½in lengths. Skin and seed the tomatoes and roughly chop the flesh into small pieces.

2 Roughly chop one of the onions and place it in a blender or food processor with the garlic, chilli, paprika, coriander and 60ml/4 tbsp water. Process to make a paste.

3 Thinly slice the second onion into rings and fry it in the oil in a pan for 5–6 minutes, until golden brown.

4 Transfer to a plate and set aside. Reduce the heat and pour the onion and coriander paste into the pan. Cook for 1–2 minutes, stirring frequently.

5 Add the okra, tomatoes, lemon juice and about 120ml/4fl oz/½ cup water. Stir well to mix, cover tightly and simmer over a low heat for about 15 minutes, until the okra is tender. Transfer to a serving dish, sprinkle with the fried onion rings and serve.

Nutritional information per portion: Energy 113kcal/471kJ; Protein 4.1g; Carbohydrate 9.2g, of which sugars 8g; Fat 7g, of which saturates 1.1g; Cholesterol 0mg; Calcium 181mg; Fibre 5.8g; Sodium 23mg.

Aubergine curry

This fiery tomato, chickpea and aubergine stew is typical of Israeli cuisine, in which vegetables such as aubergines and peppers are commonly flavoured with spices.

SERVES 4–6

about 60ml/4 tbsp olive oil

1 large aubergine (eggplant) cut into
    bitesize chunks

2 onions, thinly sliced

3–5 garlic cloves, chopped

1–2 green (bell) peppers, thinly sliced

1–2 fresh hot chillies, chopped

4 fresh or canned tomatoes, diced

30–45ml/2–3 tbsp tomato purée (paste),
    if using fresh tomatoes

5ml/1 tsp ground turmeric

pinch of curry powder or ras al hanout

cayenne pepper, to taste

400g/14oz can chickpeas, drained
    and rinsed

juice of ¹/₂–1 lemon

30–45ml/2–3 tbsp chopped fresh
    coriander (cilantro) leaves

salt

1 Heat half the oil in a frying pan, add the aubergine chunks and fry until brown, adding more oil if necessary. When cooked, transfer the aubergine chunks to a strainer, standing over a large bowl, and leave to drain thoroughly on kitchen paper.

2 Heat the remaining oil in the pan, add the onions, garlic, peppers and chillies and fry until softened.

3 Add the tomatoes, tomato purée, if using, spices and salt, and cook, stirring, until the mixture thickens. Add a little water if necessary.

4 Add the chickpeas to the sauce and cook for about 5 minutes, then add the aubergine, stir to mix well and cook for 5–10 minutes until the flavours are well combined. Add lemon juice to taste, then add the coriander leaves. Chill before serving.

Nutritional information per portion: Energy 362kcal/1536kJ; Protein 26g; Carbohydrate 60.9g, of which sugars 5.2g; Fat 3.6g, of which saturates 0.6g; Cholesterol 0mg; Calcium 117mg; Fibre 8g; Sodium 46mg.

Pineapple and coconut curry

This sweet and spicy curry benefits from being made the day before, enabling the flavours to mingle longer. In Indonesia it is often eaten at room temperature, but it is also delicious hot.

SERVES 4

1 small, firm pineapple
15–30ml/1–2 tbsp palm or coconut oil
4–6 shallots, finely chopped
2 garlic cloves, finely chopped
1 red chilli, seeded and finely chopped
15ml/1 tbsp palm sugar (jaggery)
400ml/14fl oz/1²⁄₃ cups coconut milk
salt and ground black pepper
1 small bunch fresh coriander (cilantro)
   leaves, finely chopped, to garnish

FOR THE SPICE PASTE

4 cloves
4 cardamom pods
1 small cinnamon stick
5ml/1 tsp coriander seeds
2.5ml/¹⁄₂ tsp cumin seeds
5–10ml/1–2 tsp water

1 First make the spice paste. Using a mortar and pestle or spice grinder, grind all the spices together to a powder. In a small bowl mix the spice powder with the water to make a smooth paste. Set aside.

2 Remove the skin from the pineapple then cut the flesh lengthways into quarters and remove the core. Cut each pineapple quarter widthways into chunky slices and set aside.

3 Heat the oil in a wok or large, heavy frying pan, stir in the shallots, garlic and chilli and stir-fry until fragrant and beginning to colour. Stir in the spice paste and stir-fry for 1 minute. Toss the pineapple slices into the wok, making sure they are well coated in the spicy mixture.

4 Stir the sugar into the coconut milk and pour into the wok. Bring to the boil, reduce the heat and simmer for 3–4 minutes to thicken the sauce, but don't allow the pineapple to become too soft. Season with salt and pepper.

5 Transfer the curry into a warmed serving dish and top with the coriander to garnish. Serve hot or at room temperature.

Nutritional information per portion: Energy 135kcal/573kJ; Protein 1.6g; Carbohydrate 25.4g, of which sugars 23.6g; Fat 3.8g, of which saturates 0.5g; Cholesterol 0mg; Calcium 87mg; Fibre 2.9g; Sodium 131mg.

Tamarind-laced vegetables

Fiery spices, creamy coconut, piquant tamarind and the earthy, oniony asafoetida blend together harmoniously in this dish, making it popular in southern India.

SERVES 4

125g/4¹/₂oz green beans, chopped
200g/7oz carrots, thickly slicec
225g/8oz potatoes, cubed
1 small aubergine (eggplant), chopped
2.5ml/¹/₂ tsp ground turmeric
5ml/1 tsp salt or to taste
200g/7oz cauliflower, broken into florets
10ml/2 tsp cumin seeds
50g/2oz/²/₃ cup desiccated (dry
    unsweetened shredded) coconut
2–3 green chillies, chopped
200ml/7fl oz/³/₄ cup buttermilk
30ml/2 tbsp tamarind juice
30ml/2 tbsp sunflower oil
2.5ml/¹/₂ tsp black mustard seeds
2.5ml/¹/₂ tsp cumin seeds
2–3 whole dried red chillies
6–8 curry leaves
1.5ml/¹/₄ tsp asafoetida
15ml/1 tbsp fresh coriander
    (cilantro), chopped
plain boiled basmati rice,
    to serve

1 Put the green beans, carrots, potatoes and aubergine into a pan with 350ml/12fl oz/1¹/₂ cups hot water. Add the turmeric and salt. Bring to the boil, reduce the heat to low and cover the pan. Cook for 5–6 minutes, then add the cauliflower. Cover and cook until the vegetables are tender, but still firm.

2 Meanwhile, dry-roast the 10ml/2tsp cumin seeds for 30–40 seconds. Remove from the pan and dry-roast the coconut and green chillies until lightly browned.

3 When cool, grind with the roasted cumin seeds until fine. Add the ground ingredients, buttermilk and tamarind juice to the vegetables. Cook gently for 5 minutes, then take off the heat.

4 Heat the oil and add the mustard seeds, and the 2.5ml/¹/₂tsp cumin seeds, red chillies, curry leaves and asafoetida. Blacken the chillies, then add the spices to the vegetables. Add the coriander and take off the heat. Cover and leave to stand for 5 minutes. Serve with basmati rice.

Nutritional information per portion: Energy 252kcal/1050kJ; Protein 7.55g; Carbohydrate 22.5g, of which sugars 10.7g; Fat 15.5g, of which saturates 7.7g; Cholesterol 1.75mg; Calcium 119mg; Fibre 6.1g; Sodium 57mg.

Mixed vegetables in coconut sauce

A vegetable dish is an essential part of an Indian meal, even for a simple occasion, where one or two vegetable dishes may be served with lentil dhal, raita, and bread or boiled rice.

SERVES 4

225g/8oz potatoes, cut into
    5cm/2in cubes
115g/4oz green beans
150g/5oz carrots, scraped and cut into
    5cm/2in cubes
500ml/17fl oz/2¼ cups hot water
1 small aubergine (eggplant), about
    225g/8oz, quartered lengthways
75g/3oz coconut milk powder
5ml/1 tsp salt
30ml/2 tbsp vegetable oil
6–8 fresh or 8–10 curry leaves
1 or 2 dried red chillies, chopped into
    small pieces
5ml/1 tsp ground cumin
5ml/1 tsp ground coriander
2.5ml/½ tsp ground turmeric
Indian bread, to serve

1 Put the cubed potatoes, green beans and carrots in a large pan, add 300ml/½ pint/1¼ cups of the hot water and bring to the boil. Reduce the heat a little, cover the pan and continue to cook for 5 minutes.

2 Cut the aubergine quarters into 5cm/2in pieces. Rinse. Add to the pan with the other vegetables.

3 Blend the coconut milk powder with the remaining hot water and add to the vegetables, with the salt. Bring to a slow simmer, cover and cook for 6–7 minutes.

4 In a small pan heat the oil over a medium heat and add the curry leaves and the dried red chillies. Immediately follow with the ground cumin, coriander and turmeric.

5 Stir-fry the spices together for 15–20 seconds and pour the entire contents of the pan over the vegetables. Stir to distribute the spices evenly and remove the pan from the heat.

6 Serve the mixed vegetables immediately with an Indian bread such as naan or flat bread.

Nutritional information per portion: Energy 80kcal/335kJ; Protein 1.2g; Carbohydrate 5.6g, of which sugars 5.3g; Fat 6.1g, of which saturates 0.9g; Cholesterol 0mg; Calcium 29mg; Fibre 2.3g; Sodium 71mg.

Fiery jungle curry

This fiery, flavoursome vegetarian curry is almost dominated by the chillies. This curry can be served with plain rice or noodles, or chunks of crusty bread.

SERVES 4

30ml/2 tbsp vegetable oil
2 onions, roughly chopped
2 lemon grass stalks, chopped and bruised
4 fresh green chillies, seeded and sliced
4cm/1½ in galangal or fresh root ginger, peeled and chopped
3 carrots, peeled, halved lengthways and sliced
115g/4oz yard-long beans
grated rind of 1 lime
15ml/3 tsp soy sauce
15ml/1 tbsp rice vinegar
5ml/1 tsp black peppercorns, crushed
15ml/1 tbsp sugar
10ml/2 tsp ground turmeric
115g/4oz canned bamboo shoots
75g/3oz spinach, steamed and chopped
150ml/¼ pint/⅔ cup coconut milk
chopped fresh coriander (cilantro) and mint leaves, to garnish

1 Heat a wok or heavy frying pan and add the oil. Once hot, stir in the onions, lemon grass, chillies and galangal or ginger and stir-fry for 2–3 minutes. Add the carrots and beans to the pan along with the lime rind and stir-fry for 1–2 minutes.

2 Stir in the soy sauce and rice vinegar and mix well. Add the peppercorns, sugar and turmeric.

3 Add the bamboo shoots and the chopped spinach, then stir the coconut milk into the pan and simmer over a low heat for about 10 minutes, until all the vegetables are tender.

4 Garnish with chopped fresh coriander and mint leaves and serve the curry immediately with rice, noodles or crusty bread.

Nutritional information per portion: Energy 119kcal/496kJ; Protein 3.8g; Carbohydrate 18.6g, of which sugars 15.3g; Fat 3.8g, of which saturates 0.5g; Cholesterol 0mg; Calcium 125mg; Fibre 4.3g; Sodium 60mg.

Southern Thai curried vegetables with coconut

Rich curry flavours are found in the food of Thailand, where many dishes are made with coconut milk and spiced with turmeric. Tamarind adds a tangy note.

SERVES 4

90g/3¹/₂oz **Chinese leaves (Chinese cabbage), shredded**
90g/3¹/₂oz **beansprouts**
90g/3¹/₂oz/scant 1 cup **green beans, trimmed**
100g/3¹/₂oz **broccoli florets**
15ml/1 tbsp **sesame seeds, toasted**

FOR THE SAUCE

60ml/4 tbsp **coconut cream**
5ml/1 tsp **Thai red curry paste**
90g/3¹/₂oz/1¹/₄ cups **oyster mushrooms or field (portobello) mushrooms, sliced**
60ml/4 tbsp **coconut milk**
5ml/1 tsp **ground turmeric**
5ml/1 tsp **thick tamarind juice, made by mixing tamarind paste with a little warm water**
juice of ¹/₂ lemon
60ml/4 tbsp **light soy sauce**
5ml/1 tsp **palm sugar (jaggery) or light muscovado (brown) sugar**

1 Blanch the shredded Chinese leaves, beansprouts, green beans and broccoli in boiling water for 1 minute per batch. Drain, place in a bowl and leave to cool.

2 To make the sauce, pour the coconut cream into a frying pan and heat gently for 2–3 minutes, until it separates. Stir in the red curry paste. Cook over a low heat for 30 seconds.

3 Increase the heat, add the mushrooms and cook for a further 2–3 minutes, stirring frequently. Pour in the coconut milk and stir in the turmeric, tamarind juice, lemon juice, soy sauce and sugar.

4 Pour the mixture over the prepared vegetables and toss well to combine. Sprinkle with the toasted sesame seeds and serve.

COOK'S TIP

To make coconut cream use a carton or can of coconut milk. Skim the cream off the top and cook 60ml/4 tbsp of it before adding the paste. Add the measured milk later, as in the recipe.

Nutritional information per portion: Energy 162kcal/672kJ; Protein 5g; Carbohydrate 6.3g, of which sugars 5.4g; Fat 13.2g, of which saturates 9.4g; Cholesterol 0mg; Calcium 75mg; Fibre 2.5g; Sodium 1096mg.

Pumpkin and peanut yellow curry

This is a hearty, soothing Thai curry that is perfect for autumn or winter evenings. Its cheerful colour alone will brighten you up – and it tastes terrific.

SERVES 4

30ml/2 tbsp vegetable oil

4 garlic cloves, crushed

4 shallots, finely chopped

30ml/2 tbsp Thai yellow curry paste

600ml/1 pint/2^1/$_2$ cups vegetable stock

2 kaffir lime leaves, torn

15ml/1 tbsp chopped galangal

450g/1lb pumpkin, peeled, seeded and diced

225g/8oz sweet potatoes, diced

90g/3^1/$_2$oz/scant 1 cup peanuts, roasted and chopped

300ml/^{1}/$_2$ pint/1^1/$_4$ cups coconut milk

90g/3^1/$_2$oz/1^1/$_2$ cups brown cap (cremini) mushrooms, sliced

30ml/3 tbsp light soy sauce

50g/2oz/^{1}/$_3$ cup pumpkin seeds, toasted, and fresh green chilli flowers, to garnish

1 Heat the oil in a large pan. Add the garlic and shallots and cook over a medium heat, stirring occasionally, for 10 minutes, until softened and golden. Do not let them burn.

2 Add the yellow curry paste and stir-fry over a medium heat for 30 seconds, until the mixture is fragrant. Add the stock, lime leaves, galangal, pumpkin and sweet potatoes.

3 Bring to the boil, stirring frequently, then reduce the heat to low and simmer gently for 15 minutes.

4 Add the peanuts, coconut milk and mushrooms. Add the soy sauce and simmer for about 5 minutes more. Spoon into warmed individual serving bowls, garnish with the pumpkin seeds and chilli flowers and serve.

Nutritional information per portion: Energy 306kcal/1279kJ; Protein 9.6g; Carbohydrate 24.5g, of which sugars 11.4g; Fat 19.6g, of which saturates 3.3g; Cholesterol 0mg; Calcium 160mg; Fibre 6.4g; Sodium 409mg.

Corn and cashew nut curry

This is a substantial curry, which makes a good winter-warming dish. It is deliciously aromatic, but, as the spices are added in relatively small amounts, the resulting flavour and heat is mild.

SERVES 4

30ml/2 tbsp vegetable oil

4 shallots, chopped

90g/3¹/₂ oz/scant 1 cup cashew nuts

5ml/1 tsp red curry paste

400g/14oz potatoes, peeled and cut
    into chunks

1 lemon grass stalk, finely chopped

200g/7oz can chopped tomatoes

600ml/1 pint/2¹/₂ cups boiling water

200g/7oz/generous 1 cup drained canned
    whole kernel corn

4 celery sticks, sliced

2 kaffir lime leaves, central rib removed,
    rolled into cylinders and thinly sliced

15ml/1 tbsp tomato ketchup

15ml/1 tbsp light soy sauce

5ml/1 tsp palm sugar (jaggery) or light
    muscovado (brown) sugar

4 spring onions (scallions), thinly sliced

small bunch fresh basil, roughly chopped

1 Heat the oil in a wok or deep frying pan. Add the shallots and stir-fry over a medium heat for 2–3 minutes, until softened. Add the cashew nuts to the pan and stir-fry for a few minutes until they are golden but take care not to let them burn.

2 Stir the red curry paste into the pan. Cook for 1 minute, stirring constantly, then add the potatoes, lemon grass, tomatoes and boiling water and stir well.

3 Bring back to the boil, then reduce the heat to low, cover and simmer gently for 15–20 minutes, or until the potatoes are tender when tested with the tip of a knife.

4 Stir the corn, celery, lime leaves, ketchup, soy sauce and sugar into the pan. Simmer further for about 5 minutes, until heated through, then spoon the curry into warmed serving bowls. Sprinkle with the sliced spring onions and chopped fresh basil and serve immediately.

Nutritional information per portion: Energy 298kcal/1245kJ; Protein 8.8g; Carbohydrate 27.6g, of which sugars 8.9g; Fat 17.7g, of which saturates 3.1g; Cholesterol 0mg; Calcium 33mg; Fibre 3.5g; Sodium 981mg.

Moroccan-spiced aubergine tagine

Spiced with coriander, cumin, cinnamon, turmeric and a dash of chilli sauce, this Moroccan-style spicy stew makes a filling supper dish when served with couscous.

SERVES 4

1 small aubergine (eggplant), diced
2 courgettes (zucchini), sliced
60ml/4 tbsp olive oil
1 large onion, sliced
2 garlic cloves, chopped
150g/5oz/2 cups brown cap (cremini)
     mushrooms, halved
15ml/1 tbsp ground coriander
10ml/2 tsp cumin seeds
15ml/1 tbsp ground cinnamon
10ml/2 tsp ground turmeric
225g/8oz new potatoes, quartered
600ml/1 pint/2^1/$_3$ cups passata (bottled
     strained tomatoes)
15ml/1 tbsp tomato purée (paste)
15ml/1 tbsp chilli sauce
75g/3oz/^{1}/$_2$ cup ready-to-eat
     unsulphured dried apricots
400g/14oz/3 cups canned chickpeas,
     drained and rinsed
15ml/1 tbsp chopped fresh coriander
     (cilantro), to garnish

1 Heat the grill (broiler) to high. Arrange the aubergine and courgettes on a baking tray and toss in 30ml/2 tbsp of the olive oil. Cook for 20 minutes, turning occasionally, until tender and golden.

2 Meanwhile, heat the remaining oil in a large heavy pan and cook the onion and garlic for 5 minutes until softened, stirring occasionally. Add the mushrooms and sauté for 3 minutes until tender. Add the spices and cook for 1 minute more, stirring, to allow the flavours to mingle.

3 Add the potatoes and cook for about 3 minutes, stirring. Pour in the passata, tomato purée and 150ml/^{1}/$_4$ pint/^{2}/$_3$ cup water. Cover and cook for 10 minutes to thicken the sauce.

4 Add the aubergine, courgettes, chilli sauce, apricots and chickpeas. Season and cook, partially covered, for about 15 minutes until the potatoes are tender. Add a little extra water if the tagine becomes too dry. Sprinkle with chopped fresh coriander and serve immediately.

Nutritional information per portion: Energy 359kcal/1509kJ; Protein 13.9g; Carbohydrate 45g, of which sugars 19.3g; Fat 15g, of which saturates 2.1g; Cholesterol 0mg; Calcium 123mg; Fibre 9.7g; Sodium 597mg.

Cambodian aubergine curry

Aubergine curries are popular throughout South-east Asia, the Thai version being the most famous. All are hot and aromatic, and enriched with creamy coconut milk.

SERVES 4–6

15ml/1 tbsp vegetable oil
4 garlic cloves, crushed
2 shallots, sliced
2 dried chillies
45ml/3 tbsp kroeung (hot red
    curry paste)
15ml/1 tbsp vegetable paste
15ml/1 tbsp palm sugar (jaggery)
600ml/1 pint/2¹/₂ cups coconut milk
250ml/8fl oz/1 cup vegetable stock
4 aubergines (eggplants), trimmed and
    cut into bitesize pieces
6 kaffir lime leaves
1 bunch fresh basil, stalks removed,
    leaves chopped
salt and ground black pepper
fragrant jasmine rice and 2 limes, cut into
    quarters, to serve

1 Heat the oil in a wok or heavy pan. Stir in the garlic, shallots and whole chillies and stir-fry until they begin to colour.

2 Stir in the kroeung, vegetable paste and palm sugar and stir-fry until the mixture begins to darken.

3 Pour the coconut milk and stock into the pan, and add the aubergines and lime leaves. Stir well so that all the ingredients are well combined. Bring slowly to the boil.

4 Partially cover the pan and simmer over a low heat for about 25–30 minutes until the aubergines are tender. Stir in the chopped fresh basil and check the seasoning. Serve the curry immediately with jasmine rice and lime wedges.

Nutritional information per portion: Energy 72kcal/305kJ; Protein 1.6g; Carbohydrate 11.2g, of which sugars 10.7g; Fat 3g, of which saturates 1g; Cholesterol 0mg; Calcium 46mg; Fibre 2.8g; Sodium 113mg.

Stuffed aubergines with tamarind

The traditional way of cooking with tamarind is in a terracotta dish, which brings out the full fruity tartness of the tamarind. This spicy aubergine dish will add a refreshing tang to any meal.

SERVES 4

12 baby aubergines (eggplants)
30ml/2 tbsp vegetable oil
1 small onion, chopped
10ml/2 tsp grated fresh root ginger
10ml/2 tsp crushed garlic
5ml/1 tsp coriander seeds
5ml/1 tsp cumin seeds
10ml/2 tsp white poppy seeds
10ml/2 tsp sesame seeds
10ml/2 tsp desiccated (dry unsweetened shredded) coconut
15ml/1 tbsp dry-roasted skinned peanuts
2.5–5ml/¹/₂–1 tsp chilli powder
5ml/1 tsp salt
6–8 curry leaves
1–2 dried red chillies, seeded and chopped
2.5ml/¹/₂ tsp concentrated tamarind paste

1 Make three deep slits lengthwise on each aubergine, without cutting through, then set aside.

2 Heat half the oil in a pan and fry the onion for 3–4 minutes. Add the ginger and garlic and cook for 30 seconds. Add the coriander and cumin seeds and fry for 30 seconds, then add the poppy seeds, sesame seeds and coconut. Fry for 1 minute, stirring constantly. Allow to cool slightly, then grind the spices in a food processor, adding 105ml/7 tbsp warm water.

3 Mix the peanuts, chilli powder and salt into the spice paste. Stuff each of the slits in the aubergines with the spice paste. Reserve any remaining paste.

4 Heat the remaining oil and add the curry leaves and chillies. Let the chillies blacken, then add the aubergines and the tamarind paste blended with 105ml/7 tbsp hot water. Stir in any remaining paste. Cover and simmer gently for 15–20 minutes or until the aubergines are tender. Serve.

Nutritional information per portion: Energy 132kcal/549kJ; Protein 2.9g; Carbohydrate 4.7g, of which sugars 3.8g; Fat 11.5g, of which saturates 3.3g; Cholesterol 0mg; Calcium 36mg; Fibre 3.7g; Sodium 5mg.

Vegetable korma

Korma-style was originally used for meat dishes, but many vegetarian recipes have since been created. This curry is a mixture of vegetables in a luxurious almond sauce and exotically spiced.

SERVES 4

115g/4oz fine green beans, cut into
    5cm/2in pieces
375g/13oz cauliflower, divided into
    1cm/¹/₂in florets
115g/4oz carrots, cut into batons
375g/13oz potatoes, boiled in their skins
    and cooled
50g/2oz blanched almonds, soaked in
    150ml/5fl oz/²/₃ cup boiling water
60ml/4 tbsp sunflower oil or olive oil
2 medium onions, finely chopped
2 green chillies, seeded and
    finely chopped
10ml/2 tsp ginger purée
15ml/1 tbsp ground coriander
1.5ml/¹/₄ tsp ground turmeric
2.5ml/¹/₂ tsp chilli powder
5ml/1 tsp salt, or to taste
2.5ml/¹/₂ tsp sugar
120ml/4fl oz/¹/₂ cup double
    (heavy) cream

1 Blanch all the vegetables separately – the beans for about 3 minutes, the cauliflower for 3 minutes and the carrots for 5 minutes – then plunge them immediately into cold water. Cut the cooked potatoes into 2.5cm/1in cubes.

2 Purée the blanched almonds in a blender or food processor with the water in which they were soaked, and set aside.

3 In a heavy frying pan, heat the oil over a medium heat and add the onions, green chillies and ginger purée. Fry them for 10–12 minutes, stirring regularly, until they turn a light brown colour and the onions have softened.

4 Add the coriander, turmeric and chilli powder. Reduce the heat to a low temperature and fry for 1 minute.

5 Add the vegetables, salt and sugar. Add 150ml/5fl oz/²/₃ cup warm water, stir once and then bring to the boil. Reduce the heat to low, add the cream and cook for 2–3 minutes to heat through, then serve immediately.

Nutritional information per portion: Energy 381kcal/1577kJ; Protein 5.1g; Carbohydrate 20.9g, of which sugars 9.9g; Fat 31.4g, of which saturates 19.3g; Cholesterol 78mg; Calcium 95mg; Fibre 3.9g; Sodium 108mg.

Indian-spiced parsnip curry

The sweet flavour of parsnips goes very well with the chillies and spices in this Indian-style vegetable stew. Serve it with plain yogurt and offer Indian breads to mop up the sauce.

SERVES 4

200g/7oz dried chickpeas, soaked overnight
    in cold water, then drained
7 garlic cloves, finely chopped
1 small onion, chopped
5cm/2in piece fresh root ginger, chopped
2 green chillies, seeded and chopped
75ml/5 tbsp water
450ml/³/₄ pint/scant 2 cups water
60ml/4 tbsp groundnut (peanut) oil
5ml/1 tsp cumin seeds
10ml/2 tsp ground coriander

5ml/1 tsp ground turmeric
2.5–5ml/¹/₂–1 tsp chilli powder
50g/2oz cashew nuts, toasted and ground
250g/9oz tomatoes, peeled and chopped
900g/2lb parsnips, cut in chunks
5ml/1 tsp ground cumin seeds
juice of 1 lime, to taste
salt and ground black pepper
fresh coriander (cilantro) leaves and toasted
    cashew nuts, to garnish
sour cream, to serve (optional)

1 Put the soaked chickpeas in a pan, cover with cold water and bring to the boil. Boil vigorously for 10 minutes, then reduce the heat so that the water boils steadily. Cook for 1–1¹/₂ hours, or until the chickpeas are tender. Drain.

2 Set 10ml/2 tsp of the garlic aside, then place the rest in a food processor or blender with the onion, ginger and half the green chillies. Add 75ml/5 tbsp water, and process until the mixture is smooth.

3 Heat the oil in a large, deep, frying pan and cook the cumin seeds for 30 seconds. Stir in the ground coriander, turmeric, chilli powder and the ground cashew nuts. Add the ginger and chilli paste and cook, stirring frequently. Add the tomatoes and stir-fry until the mixture begins to turn red-brown. Mix in the chickpeas and parsnips with the main batch of water, 5ml/1 tsp salt and plenty of black pepper. Bring to the boil then simmer, uncovered, for 15–20 minutes.

4 Reduce the liquid, if necessary, by boiling fiercely. Add the ground cumin with more salt and lime juice to taste. Stir in the reserved garlic and green chilli. Sprinkle the coriander leaves and toasted cashew nuts over and serve straight away with sour cream, if using.

Nutritional information per portion: Energy 506kcal/2124kJ; Protein 18.4g; Carbohydrate 60.1g, of which sugars 18.2g; Fat 23.1g, of which saturates 3.4g; Cholesterol 0mg; Calcium 192mg; Fibre 17.1g; Sodium 86mg.

Aromatic vegetable curry

Here the aim is to produce a subtle curry rather than an assault on the senses. The single chilli adds a little kick, but the warm spices and cream tend to soften the effect.

SERVES 4

50g/2oz/¹/₄ cup butter

2 onions, sliced

2 garlic cloves, crushed

2.5cm/1in piece fresh root ginger, grated

5ml/1 tsp ground cumin

15ml/1 tbsp ground coriander

6 cardamom pods

5cm/2in piece of cinnamon stick

5ml/1 tsp ground turmeric

1 fresh red chilli, seeded and chopped

1 potato, peeled and cubed

1 small aubergine (eggplant), chopped

115g/4oz/1¹/₂ cups mushrooms, sliced

175ml/6fl oz/³/₄ cup water

115g/4oz green beans, sliced

60ml/4 tbsp natural (plain) yogurt

150ml/¹/₄ pint/²/₃ cup double (heavy) cream

5ml/1 tsp garam masala

fresh coriander (cilantro) sprigs, to garnish

plain boiled rice, to serve

1 Melt the butter in a heavy pan. Add the onions and cook for 5 minutes until soft. Add the garlic and ginger and cook for 2 minutes, then stir in the cumin, coriander, cardamom pods, cinnamon stick, turmeric and finely chopped chilli. Cook, stirring constantly, for 30 seconds.

2 Add the potato cubes, aubergine and mushrooms and the water. Cover the pan, bring to the boil, then lower the heat and simmer for 15 minutes.

3 Add the beans to the pan and cook, uncovered, for about 5 minutes. With a slotted spoon, remove the vegetables to a serving dish and keep hot.

4 Allow the cooking liquid to bubble up until it has reduced a little. Season with salt and pepper to taste, then stir in the yogurt, double cream and garam masala. Pour the sauce over the vegetables and garnish with fresh coriander. Serve the curry immediately with plain boiled rice.

Nutritional information per portion: Energy 183kcal/766kJ; Protein 7g; Carbohydrate 22.7g, of which sugars 10.5g; Fat 7.9g, of which saturates 1.1g; Cholesterol 0mg; Calcium 82mg; Fibre 6.6g; Sodium 253mg.

Spicy glazed pumpkin with coconut sauce

Pumpkins, butternut squash and winter melons can all be cooked in this way. Throughout Vietnam and Cambodia, variations of this mellow dish may be served with rice or a spicy curry.

SERVES 4

200mll/7fl oz/scant 1 cup coconut milk

15ml/1 tbsp light soy sauce

30ml/2 tbsp palm sugar (jaggery)

30ml/2 tbsp groundnut (peanut) oil

4 garlic cloves, finely chopped

25g/1oz fresh root ginger, peeled and
    finely shredded

675g/1¹/₂lb pumpkin flesh, cubed

ground black pepper

a handful of curry or basil leaves,
    to garnish

chilli oil, for drizzling

fried onion rings, to garnish

plain boiled or coconut rice, to serve

1 In a bowl, beat the coconut milk and the soy sauce with the sugar, until it has dissolved. Set aside.

2 Heat the oil in a wok or heavy pan and stir in the garlic and ginger. Stir-fry until they begin to colour, then stir in the pumpkin cubes, mixing well to combine.

3 Pour in the coconut milk and mix well. Reduce the heat, cover and simmer for about 20 minutes, until the pumpkin is tender and the sauce has reduced.

4 Season with pepper and garnish with curry or basil leaves and fried onion rings. Serve hot with plain or coconut rice, drizzled with a little chilli oil.

COOK'S TIP

Curry leaves are from a type of citrus fruit tree. They release a nutty aroma in hot dishes.

Nutritional information per portion: Energy 114kcal/477kJ; Protein 1.5g; Carbohydrate 14g, of which sugars 13.4g; Fat 6g, of which saturates 1g; Cholesterol 0mg; Calcium 68mg; Fibre 1.7g; Sodium 323mg.

Tofu, green bean and mushroom red curry

This is one of those versatile recipes that should be in every curry lover's repertoire. This version uses green beans, but other types of vegetable work equally well.

SERVES 4–6

600ml/1 pint/2¹/₂ cups coconut milk
10ml/2 tsp palm sugar (jaggery)
    or honey
15ml/1 tbsp Thai red curry paste
225g/8oz/3¹/₄ cups button
    (white) mushrooms
115g/4oz green beans, trimmed
175g/6oz firm tofu, rinsed, drained and
    cut into 2cm/³/₄ in cubes
4 kaffir lime leaves, torn
2 fresh red chillies, seeded and sliced
fresh coriander (cilantro) leaves,
    to garnish

1 Pour about one-third of the coconut milk into a wok or pan. Cook until it starts to separate and an oily sheen appears on the surface of the hot liquid.

2 Add the palm sugar or honey and red curry paste to the coconut milk. Mix thoroughly, then add the mushrooms. Stir and cook for 1 minute over a medium heat.

3 Stir in the remaining coconut milk. Bring back to the boil, then add the green beans and tofu cubes. Simmer gently for 4–5 minutes more, stirring occasionally. Stir in the kaffir lime leaves and sliced red chillies.

4 Spoon the tofu and green bean curry into a serving dish, garnish with the coriander leaves and serve.

Nutritional information per portion: Energy 59kcal/250kJ; Protein 3.8g; Carbohydrate 7.5g, of which sugars 7.1g; Fat 1.8g, of which saturates 0.4g; Cholesterol 0mg; Calcium 188mg; Fibre 0.8g; Sodium 291mg.

Spicy tofu with basil and peanuts

In Vietnam, aromatic pepper leaves are used in this dish but you can use basil leaves instead. Tofu is bland, but when marinated in lemon grass, chillies and spices, it becomes a memorable dish.

SERVES 3–4

3 lemon grass stalks, finely chopped
45ml/3 tbsp soy sauce
2 red Serrano chillies, seeded and
 finely chopped
2 garlic cloves, crushed
5ml/1 tsp ground turmeric
10ml/2 tsp sugar
300g/11oz tofu, rinsed, drained, patted
 dry and cut into bitesize cubes
30ml/2 tbsp groundnut (peanut) oil
45ml/3 tbsp roasted peanuts, chopped
1 bunch fresh basil, stalks removed
salt

1 In a large mixing bowl, stir together the lemon grass, soy sauce, chopped chillies, garlic, turmeric and sugar, stirring briskly until the sugar has dissolved.

2 Add a little salt to the bowl to taste and add the tofu, making sure it is well coated in the marinade. Set aside to marinate for at least 1 hour.

3 Heat a heavy pan. Pour in the oil, add the marinated tofu, and fry, stirring, until it is golden brown on all sides. Add the peanuts and most of the basil leaves to the pan and mix well to combine the ingredients.

4 Divide the tofu among serving dishes, sprinkle with the remaining basil leaves and serve the curry.

Nutritional information per portion: Energy 120kcal/500kJ; Protein 3g; Carbohydrate 5g, of which sugars 3g; Fat 10g, of which saturates 2g; Cholesterol 0mg; Calcium 36mg; Fibre 3.3g; Sodium 200mg.

New potatoes in yogurt and poppy seed sauce

This is a rich side dish, which can also be served as a main course with Indian bread. The potatoes are partly cooked and mixed with yogurt, poppy seeds and fried onions, then finally steamed.

SERVES 4

60ml/4 tbsp sunflower oil or plain
   olive oil
700g/1½lb new potatoes, par-boiled
   and peeled
1 large onion, finely sliced
75g/3oz/⅓ cup full-fat (whole) natural
   (plain) yogurt
15ml/1 tbsp white poppy seeds, ground
5ml/1 tsp ginger purée
2.5–5ml/½–1 tsp chilli powder
5ml/1 tsp ground coriander
5ml/1 tsp ground cumin
5ml/1 tsp salt or to taste
2.5ml/½ tsp garam masala

1 Heat the oil over a medium heat and fry the potatoes in two batches until browned. Drain on kitchen paper. When they are cool enough to handle, prick the potatoes all over with a skewer to allow the flavours to penetrate.

2 In the same oil, fry the onion until it is golden. Press the onion to the side of the pan to remove any excess oil and drain on kitchen paper. Blend the yogurt, poppy seeds and fried onion in a blender to form a smooth purée and set aside. In the remaining oil in the pan, fry the ginger over a low heat for 1 minute and add the chilli powder, coriander and cumin. Stir-fry for 30–40 seconds and add the purée.

3 Cook until bubbling, then add the potatoes, salt and garam masala. Cover the pan with a piece of foil and seal the edges by pressing the foil all the way round the edge. Put the lid on and reduce the heat to very low.

4 Cook until the potatoes are tender and the sauce has thickened – about 30 minutes. Remove from the heat and serve with any Indian bread.

Nutritional information per portion: Energy 322kcal/1346kJ; Protein 7.2g; Carbohydrate 41.7g, of which sugars 10.8g; Fat 15.3g, of which saturates 2.3g; Cholesterol 2mg; Calcium 116mg; Fibre 3.8g; Sodium 41mg.

Spiced potato curry with chilli and paprika

This spicy potato curry is an Andean stew called ajiaco. It gets its name from aji, a generic word for hot pepper. The dish always combines potatoes, fresh cheese and chilli.

SERVES 6

1kg/2¼lb floury potatoes, such as
   King Edward
60ml/4 tbsp vegetable oil
6 spring onions (scallions), chopped
5ml/1 tsp grated garlic
30ml/2 tbsp chilli sauce
5ml/1 tsp paprika
250ml/8fl oz/1 cup evaporated milk
120ml/4fl oz/½ cup water
150g/5oz feta cheese
4 hard-boiled eggs, roughly chopped
salt and ground black pepper

1 Boil the potatoes in their skins in salted water for 20 minutes, until tender. Peel the potatoes and crush them lightly (they do not need to be mashed to a purée). Set aside.

2 Heat the oil in a frying pan over a medium heat and fry the spring onions and garlic for about 8 minutes, stirring frequently, until browned. Add the chilli sauce and paprika, season with salt and pepper, then stir in the potatoes, milk and water.

3 Mash the cheese with a fork and add to the potato mixture with the chopped eggs.

4 Stir with a wooden spoon and simmer for 5 minutes before serving.

Nutritional information per portion: Energy 306kcal/1281kJ; Protein 11.6g; Carbohydrate 28.7g, of which sugars 2.8g; Fat 17.1g, of which saturates 5.5g; Cholesterol 144mg; Calcium 129mg; Fibre 1.8g; Sodium 427mg.

Aloo saag

Traditional Indian spices – mustard seed, ginger and chilli – give a really good kick to potatoes and spinach in this delicious, authentic curry.

SERVES 4

450g/1lb spinach
30ml/2 tbsp vegetable oil
5ml/1 tsp black mustard seeds
1 onion, thinly sliced
2 garlic cloves, crushed
2.5cm/1in piece fresh root ginger,
   finely chopped
675g/1¹/₂lb firm potatoes, cut into
   2.5cm/1in chunks
5ml/1 tsp chilli powder
5ml/1 tsp salt
120ml/4fl oz/¹/₂ cup water

1 Wash the spinach in several changes of water then blanch it in a little boiling water for 3–4 minutes.

2 Drain the spinach thoroughly and set aside to cool slightly. When it is cool enough to handle, use your hands to squeeze out all the remaining liquid.

3 Heat the oil in a large pan and fry the mustard seeds for 2 minutes, stirring, until they begin to splutter.

4 Add the onion, garlic and ginger to the pan and cook for 5 minutes, stirring frequently.

5 Stir in the potatoes, chilli powder, salt and water and cook for about 8 minutes, stirring occasionally.

6 Finally, add the spinach to the pan. Cover and simmer for 10–15 minutes until the spinach is very soft and the potatoes are tender. Serve immediately while hot.

Nutritional information per portion: Energy 201kcal/845kJ; Protein 6.2g; Carbohydrate 30.2g, of which sugars 4.7g; Fat 6.9g, of which saturates 0.9g; Cholesterol 0mg; Calcium 205mg; Fibre 4.3g; Sodium 668mg.

Spiced chickpeas with potatoes and coriander

This dish, Chole, is made with a fragrant mix of spices, and, served garnished with tomato, raw onion, green chilli and mint, makes a sumptuous, balanced and healthy meal.

SERVES 4

60ml/4 tbsp sunflower oil
10ml/2 tsp each ginger and garlic purée
1 large onion, finely sliced
5ml/1 tsp each ground cumin and coriander
2.5ml/½ tsp ground turmeric
5ml/1 tsp chilli powder
125g/4oz can chopped tomatoes
400g/14oz/3 cups canned chickpeas
175g/6oz boiled potatoes, cubed
5ml/1 tsp salt or to taste
15ml/1tbsp lemon juice
2.5ml/½ tsp garam masala
15ml/1 tbsp each fresh coriander (cilantro)
**   and mint leaves, finely chopped**
Indian bread, to serve

TO GARNISH:
1 small tomato, seeded and sliced
1 small onion, coarsely chopped
1 fresh green chilli, deseeded and sliced
sprigs of fresh mint

1 Heat the oil over a low heat in a heavy pan and add the ginger and garlic; stir-fry for 30 seconds. Add the sliced onion, increase the heat to medium and fry for 6–7 minutes or until the onion is soft and beginning to colour.

2 Add the cumin, coriander, turmeric and chilli powder and stir-fry for 1 minute, then add the tomatoes. Cook for 3–4 minutes or until the oil begins to separate from the spiced tomato mixture.

3 Drain then add the chickpeas, potatoes, salt and 150ml/5fl oz/½ cup warm water. Bring it to the boil and reduce the heat to low. Cover and simmer for 10–12 minutes. Add the lemon juice to the chickpeas.

4 Stir in the garam masala, chopped coriander and mint leaves and remove the pan from the heat. Transfer to a serving dish and garnish with the tomato slices, onion, chilli and sprigs of mint. Serve immediately with Indian bread.

Nutritional information per portion: Energy 300kcal/1256kJ; Protein 10.1g; Carbohydrate 33.7g, of which sugars 7.5g; Fat 15g, of which saturates 1.8g; Cholesterol 0mg; Calcium 82mg; Fibre 6.2g; Sodium 232mg.

Potatoes with coriander and sun-dried mango

In this recipe, potatoes are cooked with coriander seeds, chillies and and sun-dried mango powder, which has a sour taste. If it proves difficult to find, lime juice can be used instead.

SERVES 4

60ml/4 tbsp sunflower oil or plain olive oil

1 large onion, finely sliced

1–2 green chillies, chopped (seeded
    if you like)

1–2 dried red chillies, each sliced into
    2–3 pieces

10ml/2 tsp coriander seeds, crushed

5ml/1 tsp ground cumin

2.5ml/1/2 tsp ground turmeric

450g/1lb potatoes, cut into
    2.5cm/1in cubes

5ml/1 tsp salt or to taste

5ml/1 tsp sun-dried mango powder
    (amchur) or 1 tbsp lime juice

30ml/2 tbsp coriander (cilantro)
    leaves, chopped

1 Heat the oil and fry the onion with the green and red chillies, until the onion begins to brown.

2 Add the crushed coriander and stir-fry for about a minute. Add the cumin and turmeric, stir-fry for about a minute, then add the potatoes and salt. Add 250ml/ 9fl oz/1 cup warm water and bring it to the boil.

3 Reduce the heat to low, cover the pan and cook for 12–15 minutes until the potatoes are tender and all the water has been absorbed.

4 Stir in the mango powder or lime juice and coriander leaves, and remove from the heat. Serve with a lentil dish and/or a vegetable curry, accompanied by any type of Indian bread.

Nutritional information per portion: Energy 237kcal/990kJ; Protein 4.2g; Carbohydrate 29.7g, of which sugars 8.5g; Fat 12.2g, of which saturates 1.5g; Cholesterol 0mg; Calcium 47mg; Fibre 2.9g; Sodium 509mg.

Potatoes in chilli tamarind sauce

In this potato dish from southern India, the mix of chilli and tamarind tingles the taste buds. This version adapts the classic recipe, to reduce the pungency and enhance the fiery appearance.

SERVES 4–6

450g/1lb small new potatoes, washed
   and dried
25g/1oz whole dried red chillies
7.5ml/1½ tsp cumin seeds
4 garlic cloves
90ml/6 tbsp vegetable oil
60ml/4 tbsp thick tamarind juice, made
   by mixing tamarind paste with
   warm water
30ml/2 tbsp tomato purée (paste)
4 curry leaves
5ml/1 tsp sugar
1.5ml/¼ tsp asafoetida
salt
coriander (cilantro) sprigs and lemon
   wedges, to garnish

1 Cook the potatoes in a large pan of salted water for 12–15 minutes, or until just cooked, ensuring they do not break. To test, insert a thin sharp knife into the potatoes. Drain them and place in a bowl of iced water to prevent further cooking.

2 Soak the chillies for 5 minutes in warm water. Drain and grind with the cumin seeds and garlic to a coarse paste either using a mortar and pestle or in a food processor.

3 Heat the oil in a wok or deep frying pan and fry the spice paste, tamarind juice, tomato purée, curry leaves, salt, sugar and asafoetida until the oil separates from the spice paste.

4 Drain the the potatoes and add to the pan. Reduce the heat to low, cover the pan with a lid and simmer the potatoes for 5 minutes. Garnish with coriander and lemon wedges and serve immediately.

Nutritional information per portion: Energy 90kcal/379kJ; Protein 2.7g; Carbohydrate 19.5g, of which sugars 5.7g; Fat 0.7g, of which saturates 0.1g; Cholesterol 0mg; Calcium 30mg; Fibre 1.9g; Sodium 12mg.

Potatoes in aromatic sauce

In this dish, small new potatoes are fried in mustard oil, which adds a superbly nutty, mellow flavour. They are then spiced and simmered in a yogurt sauce.

SERVES 4

60ml/4 tbsp mustard oil

700g/1¹/₂lb small potatoes, boiled
    and peeled

2.5–5ml/¹/₂–1 tsp chilli powder

2 brown cardamom pods, bruised

4 green cardamom pods, bruised

2.5ml/¹/₂ tsp ground ginger

5ml/1 tsp ground coriander

5ml/1 tsp ground fennel

5ml/1 tsp salt or to taste

150g/5oz/¹/₂ cup natural (plain)
    yogurt, whisked

1 In a medium-sized pan, heat the oil until smoking and fry the potatoes in two batches until they are well browned. Take the pan off the heat and drain the potatoes on kitchen paper. When they are cool enough to handle, prick the potatoes all over to allow the flavours to penetrate.

2 Place the pan back over a low heat and add the chilli powder, followed by 30ml/2 tbsp water. Cook for 1 minute and add all the remaining spices. Cook for a further minute.

3 Add the browned potatoes, salt and yogurt. Cover the pan tightly and reduce the heat to low. Cook until the sauce thickens and coats the potatoes (5–6 minutes). Remove from the heat and serve with naan bread or chapatis.

Nutritional information per portion: Energy 261kcal/1092kJ; Protein 5.8g; Carbohydrate 33.2g, of which sugars 5.1g; Fat 12.7g, of which saturates 1.8g; Cholesterol 1mg; Calcium 93mg; Fibre 1.8g; Sodium 53mg.

Cauliflower, pea and potato curry

This highly spiced vegetable curry is often prepared for religious festivals and other special occasions in India. It also makes a delicious light lunch.

SERVES 4

500g/1¼lb potatoes

1 small cauliflower or 350g/12oz cauliflower florets, with outer stalks removed

45ml/3 tbsp sunflower oil or olive oil

1 large onion, finely sliced

5ml/1 tsp ginger purée

5ml/1 tsp garlic purée

2 green chillies, chopped and seeded

2.5ml/½ tsp ground turmeric

5ml/1 tsp ground coriander

175g/6oz fresh tomatoes, chopped

5ml/1 tsp salt, or to taste

115g/4oz frozen garden peas

15ml/1 tbsp chopped fresh coriander (cilantro), to garnish

1 Halve or quarter the potatoes – the pieces should be quite chunky so that they do not fall apart during cooking. Divide the cauliflower into 2.5cm/1in florets, then blanch them briefly and plunge them in cold water.

2 Heat the oil in a large, non-stick pan over a medium to high heat and brown the potatoes in two to three batches until they are well browned and form a crust on the surface – they will look a little like roast potatoes. Drain them thoroughly on absorbent kitchen paper.

3 In the same oil, fry the onion, ginger, garlic and chillies over a low to medium heat, stirring regularly, for 6–8 minutes or until the mixture begins to brown. Add the ground turmeric and coriander, cook for 1 minute and then add the tomatoes, fried potatoes and salt.

4 Pour in 400ml/14fl oz/1⅔ cups warm water. Bring this to the boil, reduce the heat to low, then cover and cook for 15 minutes. Drain the cauliflower and add to the pan with the coated potato mixture. Add the peas, cook for 5 minutes. Remove from the heat and serve, garnished with coriander.

Nutritional information per portion: Energy 276kcal/1153kJ; Protein 9.7g; Carbohydrate 37g, of which sugars 11.6g; Fat 10.9g, of which saturates 1.5g; Cholesterol 0mg; Calcium 89mg; Fibre 6.5g; Sodium 33.8mg.

Egg, potato and green pea curry

In this classic dish, hard-boiled eggs and cubed boiled potatoes are flavoured with turmeric and chilli powder and shallow-fried to a rich golden colour then simmered in an aromatic sauce.

SERVES 4

4 hard-boiled eggs
350g/12oz medium-sized potatoes, peeled
   and quartered
60ml/4 tbsp sunflower oil or plain olive oil
2.5ml/¹/₂ tsp ground turmeric
2.5ml/¹/₂ tsp chilli powder
2.5cm/1in piece of cinnamon stick
4 green cardamom pods, bruised
4 cloves
2 bay leaves

1 large onion, finely chopped
5ml/1 tsp ground coriander
2.5ml/¹/₂ tsp ground cumin
1 fresh tomato, skinned and chopped
5ml/1 tsp salt or to taste
2.5ml/¹/₂ tsp sugar
115g/4oz/1 cup frozen peas, thawed, or
   pre-cooked fresh peas
2.5ml/¹/₂ tsp garam masala

1 Shell the eggs and make four small slits in each without cutting them right through. Wash the potatoes and dry them with a cloth.

2 Heat the oil over a low heat and add 1.5ml/¹/₄ tsp each of the turmeric and chilli powder, then the whole eggs. Move the eggs until they are coloured by the spices and develop a light golden crust. Remove the eggs and set them aside.

3 Add the potatoes to the same oil and increase the heat to medium. Stir-fry them until they are well browned and develop a light golden crust. Remove them with a slotted spoon and drain on kitchen paper.

4 Reduce the heat to low and add the cinnamon, cardamom, cloves and bay leaves and fry them for a few seconds. Add the onion, increase the heat to medium, and fry until the onion is golden brown (9–10 minutes). On a low heat, add the coriander and cumin and the remaining turmeric and chilli powder. Stir-fry for 1 minute, then add the tomato and continue to cook for 1–2 minutes.

5 Add the potatoes, salt and sugar, and 250ml/8fl oz/1 cup warm water. Bring to the boil, cover the pan and reduce the heat to low. Cook until the potatoes are al dente. Add the peas, cover and cook for 5–6 minutes longer, until the potatoes are tender and the peas are cooked. Stir in the garam masala and remove from the heat. Serve with Indian bread.

Nutritional information per portion: Energy 316kcal/1317kJ; Protein 11.9g; Carbohydrate 29g, of which sugars 9.3g; Fat 18g, of which saturates 3.1g; Cholesterol 190mg; Calcium 79mg; Fibre 4.2g; Sodium 87mg.

Cheese with mushrooms and peas

An Indian cheese, paneer, is used in both sweet and savoury dishes. In India this cheese is often made at home, although it has now become available in supermarkets and Indian stores.

SERVES 4–6

90ml/6 tbsp ghee or vegetable oil
225g/8oz paneer, cubed
1 onion, finely chopped
a few fresh mint leaves, chopped, plus extra sprigs to garnish
50g/2oz chopped fresh coriander (cilantro)
3 fresh green chillies, chopped
3 garlic cloves
2.5cm/1in piece fresh root ginger, sliced
5ml/1 tsp ground turmeric
5ml/1 tsp chilli powder (optional)
5ml/1 tsp garam masala
225g/8oz/3 cups tiny button (white) mushrooms, washed
225g/8oz/2 cups frozen peas, thawed
175ml/6fl oz/³⁄₄ cup natural (plain) yogurt, mixed with 5ml/1 tsp cornflour (cornstarch)
salt

1 Heat the ghee or oil in a wok, karahi or large pan, and fry the paneer cubes until they are golden brown on all sides. Remove, drain on kitchen paper, and keep to one side.

2 Grind the onion, mint, coriander, chillies, garlic and ginger in a mortar or in a food processor or blender to a fairly smooth paste.

3 Remove to a bowl and mix in the turmeric, chilli powder, if using, and garam masala, and season with salt.

4 Remove excess ghee or oil from the pan, leaving about 15ml/1 tbsp. Heat and fry the paste over a medium heat for 8–10 minutes, or until the oil separates. Add the mushrooms, thawed peas and paneer, and mix well. Cool the mixture slightly and gradually fold in the yogurt.

5 Simmer for about 10 minutes, until the vegetables are tender. Serve immediately, garnished with sprigs of fresh mint.

Nutritional information per portion: Energy 294kcal/1217kJ; Protein 14.4g; Carbohydrate 14g, of which sugars 7.3g; Fat 20.3g, of which saturates 3.7g; Cholesterol 10mg; Calcium 174mg; Fibre 3.5g; Sodium 210mg.

Potato curry with yogurt

Variations of this simple Indian curry are popular in Singapore, where fusion dishes like this cater for a community that includes people from all over Asia, as well as from Europe and the Americas.

SERVES 4

6 garlic cloves, chopped

25g/1oz fresh root ginger, peeled and chopped

30ml/2 tbsp ghee, or 15ml/1 tbsp oil and 15g/1/2oz/1 tbsp butter

6 shallots, halved lengthways and sliced

2 fresh green chillies, seeded and sliced

10ml/2 tsp sugar

a handful of fresh or dried curry leaves

2 cinnamon sticks

5–10ml/1–2 tsp ground turmeric

15ml/1 tbsp garam masala

500g/1¼lb waxy potatoes, cubed

2 tomatoes, peeled, seeded and quartered

250ml/8fl oz/1 cup Greek (US strained plain) yogurt

salt and ground black pepper

5ml/1 tsp red chilli powder, and fresh coriander (cilantro) and mint leaves, finely chopped, to garnish

1 lemon, cut into quarters, to serve

1 Using a mortar and pestle or a food processor, grind the garlic and ginger to a coarse paste.

2 Heat the ghee or oil and butter in a heavy pan and stir in the shallots and chillies, until fragrant. Add the garlic and ginger paste with the sugar, and stir until the mixture begins to colour. Stir in the curry leaves, cinnamon sticks, turmeric and garam masala, and toss in the potatoes, making sure they are well coated in the spice mixture.

3 Add enough cold water to the pan to cover the potatoes. Bring to the boil, reduce the heat and simmer until the potatoes are just cooked – they should still have a bite rather than being mushy.

4 Season with salt and pepper to taste. Gently toss in the tomatoes to heat them through. Fold in the yogurt so that it is streaky. Sprinkle with the chilli powder, coriander and mint. Serve immediately from the pan, with lemon to squeeze over.

Nutritional information per portion: Energy 231kcal/967kJ; Protein 6.7g; Carbohydrate 26.2g, of which sugars 7.4g; Fat 12.4g, of which saturates 4.1g; Cholesterol 0mg; Calcium 110mg; Fibre 2g; Sodium 63mg.

Cinnamon and clove-scented cheese curry

Indian cheese (paneer) is a great source of protein for vegetarians, and the vast majority of the population thrive on this versatile ingredient, which is used for savoury and sweet dishes.

SERVES 4

60ml/4 tbsp sunflower oil or plain olive oil

225g/8oz/2 cups paneer, cut into
    2.5cm/1in cubes

400g/14oz potatoes, cut into
    2.5cm/1in cubes

2.5cm/1in piece of cinnamon stick

4 green cardamom pods, bruised

4 cloves

1 large onion, finely chopped

5ml/1 tsp ginger purée

5ml/1 tsp garlic purée

2.5ml/^{1}/$_2$ tsp ground turmeric

2.5–5ml/^{1}/$_2$–1 tsp chilli powder

2.5ml/^{1}/$_2$ tsp ground cumin

5ml/1 tsp salt or to taste

2.5ml/^{1}/$_2$ tsp garam masala

15ml/1 tbsp coriander (cilantro) leaves,
    chopped

1 Heat half the oil in a non-stick pan over a medium heat and brown the cubes of paneer. Stand well away from the pan while frying the paneer as it tends to splutter. Drain the cubes on kitchen paper. Dry the cubes of potato with a cloth and brown them in the same oil. Drain on kitchen paper.

2 Add the remaining oil to the pan and reduce the heat to low. Add the cinnamon, cardamom and cloves; let them sizzle until the cardamom pods have puffed up. Add the onion and increase the heat slightly. Cook for 5–6 minutes until the onion has softened, then add the ginger and garlic and fry until the onion is beginning to brown. Add the turmeric, chilli powder and cumin and cook for about a minute. Next, add 30ml/2 tbsp water, and cook until the mixture is dry and the water has evaporated. Repeat this process twice more (adding 90ml/6 tbsp water in all).

3 Add the browned potatoes, salt and 250ml/8fl oz/1 cup warm water to the pan. Bring the mixture to the boil, reduce the heat to low, cover and simmer for 10 minutes. Add the browned paneer, increase the heat to medium and cook uncovered for 5–6 minutes until the sauce thickens.

4 Add the garam masala and coriander leaves, stir well and remove from the heat. Serve with any Indian bread.

Nutritional information per portion: Energy 280kcal/1170kJ; Protein 11.5g; Carbohydrate 28.5g, of which sugars 9.5g; Fat 14.2g, of which saturates 2.9g; Cholesterol 7mg; Calcium 85mg; Fibre 2.8g; Sodium 230mg.

Onion bhajiyas

One of the most popular snacks in India, onion bhajiyas come in several versions. Bhajiyas are delicious served on their own or accompanied by a chutney of your choice.

SERVES 4–6

150g/5oz/1¼ cups gram flour, sifted
25g/1oz ground rice
5ml/1 tsp salt or to taste
pinch of bicarbonate of soda
   (baking soda)
2.5ml/½ tsp ground turmeric
5ml/1 tsp ground cumin
5ml/1 tsp cumin seeds
2.5ml/½ tsp asafoetida
2 green chillies, finely chopped (seeded if
   you like)
450g/1lb onions, sliced into half rings
   and separated
15g/½oz coriander (cilantro) leaves and
   stalks, finely chopped
sunflower oil or plain olive oil for
   deep-frying

1 Mix together the flour, ground rice, salt, bicarbonate of soda, turmeric, ground cumin, cumin seeds and asafoetida. Add the chillies, onion rings and coriander. Gradually pour in 200ml/7fl oz/¾ cup water and mix until a thick batter is formed and all the ingredients are well coated.

2 In a wok or pan for deep-frying, heat the oil over a medium heat, ensuring the temperature reaches at least 180°C/350°F if you have a thermometer. The temperature of the oil is crucial – if it is not hot enough the bhajiyas will be soggy. To measure the temperature without a thermometer, drop about 1.5ml/¼ tsp of the batter into the hot oil. If it floats up to the surface immediately without turning brown, then the oil is at the right temperature.

3 Lower about 15ml/1 tbsp at a time of the onion batter mix into the hot oil, in a single layer. Avoid overcrowding the pan or the bhajiyas will not crisp up. Reduce the heat slightly and continue to cook until the bhajiyas are golden and crisp. Maintaining a steady temperature is important to ensure that the centre of each bhajiya is cooked and the outside turns brown. This should take 8–10 minutes. Drain on kitchen paper and serve with chutney.

Nutritional information per portion: Energy 284kcal/1181kJ; Protein 5.1g; Carbohydrate 27g, of which sugars 4.7g; Fat 18g, of which saturates 1.9g; Cholesterol 0mg; Calcium 38mg; Fibre 3.3g; Sodium 5mg.

Vegetable samosas

Throughout the East, these spicy parcels are sold by street vendors, and eaten at any time of day.
They make a great snack for lunch boxes, or whenever you are on the move.

MAKES ABOUT 20

1 packet 25cm/10in square spring roll
   wrappers, thawed if frozen
30ml/2 tbsp plain (all-purpose) flour,
   mixed to a paste with a little water
vegetable oil, for deep-frying
coriander (cilantro) leaves, to garnish

FOR THE FILLING

25g/1oz/2 tbsp ghee or unsalted butter
1 small onion, finely chopped
1cm/½in fresh root ginger, chopped
1 garlic clove, crushed
2.5ml/½ tsp chilli powder
1 potato, 225g/8oz, cooked and diced
50g/2oz/½ cup cauliflower florets,
   lightly cooked and chopped
50g/2oz/½ cup frozen peas, thawed
5–10ml/1–2 tsp garam masala
15ml/1 tbsp chopped fresh coriander
   (cilantro) leaves and stems
squeeze of lemon juice and salt

1 To make the filling, heat the ghee or butter in a large frying pan and fry the onion, ginger and garlic for 5 minutes until the onion has softened but not browned.

2 Add the chilli powder and cook for 1 minute, then stir in the potato, cauliflower and peas. Sprinkle with garam masala and set aside to cool. Stir in the coriander, lemon juice and salt.

3 Cut the spring roll wrappers into three equal strips (or two for larger samosas). Brush the edges with a little of the flour paste. Place a small spoonful of filling about 2cm/¾in in from the edge of one strip. Fold one corner over the filling to make a triangle and continue this folding until the entire strip has been used and a triangular pastry has been formed. Seal any open edges with more flour and water paste.

4 Heat the oil for deep-frying to 190°C/375°F and fry the samosas, a few at a time, until golden and crisp. Drain well on kitchen paper and serve hot, garnished with coriander leaves.

Nutritional information per portion: Energy 56kcal/235kJ; Protein 1.3g; Carbohydrate 10g, of which sugars 0.8g; Fat 1.4g, of which saturates 0.2g; Cholesterol 0mg; Calcium 16mg; Fibre 0.7g; Sodium 8mg.

Pea and potato pakoras with coconut and mint chutney

These delicious golden bites are crisp batter balls with a fragrant centre of spicy vegetables. Pakoras are sold as street food throughout India, and make a wonderful snack drizzled with the fragrant chutney, or you could sandwich them in a crusty roll for a light lunch.

MAKES 25

15ml/1 tbsp sunflower oil
20ml/4 tsp cumin seeds
5ml/1 tsp black mustard seeds
1 small onion, finely chopped
10ml/2 tsp grated fresh root ginger
2 green chillies, seeded and chopped
600g/1lb 5oz potatoes, peeled, diced and
   boiled until tender
200g/7oz fresh peas
juice of 1 lemon
90ml/6 tbsp chopped fresh coriander
   (cilantro) leaves
115g/4oz/1 cup besan (chickpea flour)
25g/1oz/¼ cup self-raising
   (self-rising) flour

40g/1½oz/⅓ cup rice flour
 large pinch of turmeric
10ml/2 tsp crushed coriander seeds
350ml/12fl oz/1½ cups water
vegetable oil, for frying
salt and ground black pepper

FOR THE CHUTNEY
105ml/7 tbsp coconut cream
200ml/7fl oz/scant 1 cup natural
   (plain) yogurt
50g/2oz mint leaves, finely chopped
5ml/1 tsp golden caster (superfine) sugar
juice of 1 lime

1 Heat a wok over a medium heat and add the sunflower oil. When hot, add the cumin and mustard seeds and stir-fry for 1–2 minutes.

2 Add the onion, ginger and chillies to the wok and cook for 3–4 minutes. Add the cooked potatoes and peas and stir-fry for 3-4 minutes. Season, then stir in the lemon juice and coriander leaves.

3 Leave the mixture to cool slightly, then divide into 25 portions. Shape each portion into a ball and chill.

4 To make the batter put the besan, self-raising flour and rice flour in a bowl. Season and add the turmeric and coriander seeds. Gradually whisk in the water to make a smooth, thick batter.

5 To make the chutney place all the ingredients in a blender and process until smooth. Season, then chill until ready to serve.

6 To cook the pakoras, fill a wok one-third full of oil and heat to 180°C/350°F. (A cube of bread, dropped into the oil, should brown in 15 seconds.) Working in batches, dip the balls in the batter, then drop into the oil and deep-fry for 1–2 minutes, or until golden. Drain on kitchen paper and serve with the chutney.

COOK'S TIP
Besan, also known as gram flour, is a fine yellow flour made from ground chickpeas. Widely used in Asian cooking, it is available in most large supermarkets and Asian stores.

Nutritional information per portion: Energy 126kcal/525kJ; Protein 4.1g; Carbohydrate 8.3g, of which sugars 2.6g; Fat 8.8g, of which saturates 5.2g; Cholesterol 0mg; Calcium 35mg; Fibre 1.3g; Sodium 16mg.

Rice Dishes

Rice is a perfect partner for a curry, it can temper the heat of chillies, and adds its own unique flavour to a spicy dish. Long-grain scented rice has a delicate fragrant taste and often accompanies Thai curries; while basmati rice has a wonderful aroma that complements Indian curries. More substantial rice dishes can stand alone – try Chicken Biryani, Spiced Lamb and Vegetable Pilau, or Vegetarian Kedgeree.

Saffron rice

The saffron crocus only flowers for two weeks of the year, and each stigma has to be removed by hand and dried with care. Consequently, saffron is said to be worth its weight in gold.

SERVES 6

450g/1lb/2¹/₃ cups basmati rice, soaked
    for 20–30 minutes
750ml/1¹/₄ pints/3 cups water
3 green cardamom pods
2 cloves
5ml/1 tsp salt
45ml/3 tbsp semi-skimmed
    (low-fat) milk
2.5ml/¹/₂ tsp saffron threads, crushed

1 Drain the basmati rice and place in a large pan. Pour in the water. Add the cardamoms, cloves and salt. Stir, then bring to the boil. Lower the heat and cover tightly, and simmer for 5 minutes.

2 Meanwhile, place the milk in a small pan. Add the saffron threads and heat through gently.

3 Add the saffron milk to the rice and stir. Cover again and continue cooking over a low heat for 5–6 minutes.

4 Remove the pan from the heat without lifting the lid. Leave the rice to stand for about 5 minutes, then fork through just before serving.

Nutritional information per portion: Energy 348Kcal/1452kJ; Protein 6.7g; Carbohydrate 71g, of which sugars 0.9g; Fat 3.6g, of which saturates 2g; Cholesterol 8mg; Calcium 21mg; Fibre 0.2g; Sodium 515mg.

Caramelized basmati rice

This is the traditional accompaniment to a dhansak curry. Sugar is caramelized in hot oil before the rice is added, along with a few whole spices.

SERVES 4

225g/8oz/generous 1 cup basmati rice,
    washed and soaked for 20–30 minutes
45ml/3 tbsp vegetable oil
20ml/4 tsp granulated (white) sugar
4–5 green cardamom pods, bruised
2.5cm/1in piece cinnamon stick
4 cloves
1 bay leaf, crumbled
½ tsp salt
475ml/16fl oz/2 cups hot water

1 Put the basmati rice in a colander and leave to drain.

2 In a large pan, heat the vegetable oil over a medium heat. When the oil is hot, add the granulated sugar and wait until it is caramelized.

3 Reduce the heat to low and add the spices and bay leaf. Let it sizzle for about 15–20 seconds, then add the rice and salt. Fry gently, stirring, for 2–3 minutes.

4 Pour in the water and bring to the boil. Let it boil steadily for 2 minutes then reduce the heat to very low. Cover the pan and cook for 8 minutes.

5 Remove the rice from the heat and let it stand for 6–8 minutes. Gently fluff up the rice with a fork and transfer to a warmed dish to serve.

Nutritional information per portion: Energy 324Kcal/1353kJ; Protein 4.1g; Carbohydrate 56.4g, of which sugars 12.5g; Fat 9.1g, of which saturates 2g; Cholesterol 53mg; Calcium 41mg; Fibre 0.5g; Sodium 212mg.

Aromatic Indian pilaff with peas

This fragrant, versatile rice dish is often served as part of an elaborate meal at Indian festivals and celebratory feasts, which include several meat and vegetable curries, a yogurt dish, and chutneys. On occasion, ground turmeric or grated carrot is added for an extra splash of colour. Sprinkle the pilaff with chopped fresh mint and coriander (cilantro), if you like, or add some roasted chilli and coconut.

SERVES 4

350g/12oz/1¾ cups basmati rice
45ml/3 tbsp ghee or 30ml/2 tbsp vegetable
   oil and a little butter
1 cinnamon stick
6–8 cardamom pods, crushed
4 cloves

1 onion, halved lengthways and sliced
25g/1oz fresh root ginger, peeled and grated
5ml/1 tsp sugar
130g/4½oz fresh peas, shelled
5ml/1 tsp salt

1 Rinse the rice and put it in a bowl. Cover with plenty of water and leave to soak for 30 minutes. Drain thoroughly.

2 Heat the ghee, or oil and butter, in a heavy pan. Stir in the cinnamon stick, cardamom and cloves. Add the onion, ginger and sugar, and fry until golden. Add the peas, followed by the rice, and stir for 1 minute to coat the rice in ghee or oil and butter.

3 Pour in 600ml/1 pint/2½ cups water with the salt, stir once and bring the liquid to the boil. Reduce the heat and allow to simmer for 15–20 minutes, until all the liquid has been absorbed.

4 Turn off the heat, cover the pan with a clean dishtowel and the lid, and leave the rice to steam for a further 10 minutes. Spoon the rice on to a serving dish.

VARIATION

This Indian pilaff also works with diced carrot or beetroot (beet), or chickpeas. Instead of turmeric, you can add a little tomato paste to give the rice a red tinge.

Nutritional information per portion: Energy 451Kcal/1880kJ; Protein 8.9g; Carbohydrate 75.7g, of which sugars 2.6g; Fat 12.2g, of which saturates 5.4g; Cholesterol 0mg; Calcium 28mg; Fibre 1.8g; Sodium 328mg.

Coconut rice

This snow-white basmati rice, speckled with black mustard seeds and dotted with red chilli pieces, looks quite stunning. It is best served with a simple lentil dish or a vegetable curry.

SERVES 4

225g/8oz/generous 1 cup basmati rice
5ml/1 tsp salt or to taste
50g/2oz/²⁄₃ cup desiccated (dry unsweetened shredded) coconut
125ml/4fl oz/¹⁄₂ cup milk
30ml/2 tbsp sunflower oil or plain olive oil
50g/2oz/¹⁄₂ cup raw cashew nuts
2.5ml/¹⁄₂ tsp black mustard seeds
15ml/1 tbsp skinless split chickpeas (channa dhal)
2–3 dried red chillies
8–10 curry leaves

1 Wash the rice until the water runs clear, then leave it to soak for 20 minutes. Drain and put it into a heavy pan. Pour in 450ml/16fl oz/ scant 2 cups hot water. Stir in the salt and bring it to the boil. Let it boil for 2 minutes, then turn the heat down to very low, cover the pan and cook for 8 minutes without lifting the lid. Remove from the heat and let the pan stand undisturbed for 8–10 minutes.

2 Meanwhile, put the coconut into a small pan and add the milk. Stir over low to medium heat until the coconut has absorbed all the milk. This enriches the dried coconut, giving it a luscious taste.

3 Heat the oil in a small pan or a steel ladle over a low heat and brown the cashew nuts. Drain on kitchen paper. Increase the heat to medium and when the oil is fairly hot, but not smoking, add the mustard seeds, split chickpeas, red chillies and curry leaves (in that order). Allow the seeds to pop and the chillies to blacken slightly. Pour the entire contents of the pan over the rice and add the coconut and cashew nuts. Gently mix with a fork and serve.

Nutritional information per portion: Energy 436kcal/1813kJ; Protein 9.3g; Carbohydrate 51.7g, of which sugars 3.1g; Fat 21.2g, of which saturates 9.4g; Cholesterol 4mg; Calcium 56mg; Fibre 2.3g; Sodium 58mg.

Herby rice pilau

Serve this simple pilau with a main course meat, poultry or vegetarian curry accompanied by a selection of fresh seasonal vegetables such as broccoli florets, baby corn, asparagus and carrots.

SERVES 4

1 onion
1 garlic clove
225g/8oz/generous 1 cup mixed brown
    basmati and wild rice
15ml/1 tbsp olive oil
5ml/1 tsp ground cumin
5ml/1 tsp ground turmeric
50g/2oz/¹/₃ cup sultanas (golden raisins)
750ml/1¹/₄ pints/3 cups vegetable stock
30–45ml/2–3 tbsp chopped fresh
    mixed herbs
salt and ground black pepper
sprigs of fresh herbs and 25g/1oz/¹/₄ cup
    pistachio nuts, chopped, to garnish

1 Chop the onion and crush the garlic cloves.

2 Wash the rice under cold running water until the water runs clear, then drain well.

3 Heat the oil, add the onion and garlic, and cook gently for 5 minutes, stirring occasionally.

4 Add the ground cumin and turmeric and drained rice and cook gently for 1 minute, stirring. Stir in the sultanas and vegetable stock, bring to the boil, cover and simmer gently for 20–25 minutes, stirring occasionally.

5 Stir in the chopped mixed herbs and season with salt and pepper to taste.

6 Spoon the pilau into a warmed serving dish and garnish with fresh herb sprigs and a sprinkling of chopped pistachio nuts. Serve immediately.

Nutritional information per portion:Energy 288kcal/1218kJ; Protein 5g; Carbohydrate 58g, of which sugars 12g; Fat 6g, of which saturates 1g; Cholesterol 0mg; Calcium 30mg; Fibre 3g; Sodium 321mg.

Nut pilau

Versions of this rice dish are cooked throughout Asia, always with the best-quality long grain rice. In India, basmati rice is the natural choice. In this particular interpretation of the recipe, walnuts and cashew nuts are added. Serve the pilau with a raita or yogurt.

SERVES 4

15–30ml/1–2 tbsp vegetable oil

1 onion, chopped

1 garlic clove, crushed

1 large carrot, coarsely grated

225g/8oz/generous 1 cup basmati rice,
　　soaked for 20–30 minutes

5ml/1 tsp cumin seeds

10ml/2 tsp ground coriander

10ml/2 tsp black mustard seeds

4 green cardamom pods

450ml/³⁄₄ pint/scant 2 cups
　　vegetable stock

1 bay leaf

75g/3oz/³⁄₄ cup unsalted walnuts and
　　cashew nuts

salt and ground black pepper

fresh coriander (cilantro) sprigs, to
　　garnish

1 Heat the oil in a karahi, wok or large pan. Fry the onion, garlic and carrot for 3–4 minutes. Drain the rice and add to the pan with the spices. Cook for 2 minutes, stirring to coat the grains in oil.

2 Pour in the stock, stirring. Add the bay leaf and season well.

3 Bring to the boil, lower the heat, cover and simmer very gently for 10–12 minutes without stirring.

4 Remove the pan from the heat without lifting the lid. Leave to stand for 5 minutes, then check the rice. If it is cooked, there will be small steam holes on the surface of the rice. Discard the bay leaf and the cardamom pods.

5 Stir in the walnuts and cashew nuts and check the seasoning. Spoon on to a warmed platter, garnish with the fresh coriander and serve.

Nutritional information per portion: Energy 370kcal/1538kJ; Protein 7.3g; Carbohydrate 48.7g, of which sugars 3.2g; Fat 16g, of which saturates 1.4g; Cholesterol 0mg; Calcium 38mg; Fibre 1.5g; Sodium 8mg.

Sultana and cashew pilau

The secret of a perfect pilau is to wash the rice thoroughly, then soak it briefly. This softens and moistens the grains, enabling the rice to absorb moisture during cooking, which results in fluffier rice. This tasty pilau would be perfect for a light lunch or supper.

SERVES 4

600ml/1 pint/2¹/₂ cups hot chicken stock
generous pinch of saffron threads
50g/2oz/¹/₄ cup butter
1 onion, chopped
1 garlic clove, crushed
2.5cm/1in piece cinnamon stick
6 green cardamom pods
1 bay leaf
250g/9oz/1¹/₃ cups basmati rice, soaked
    in water for 20–30 minutes
50g/2oz/¹/₃ cup sultanas (golden raisins)
15ml/1 tbsp vegetable oil
50g/2oz/¹/₂ cup cashew nuts
naan bread and tomato and onion salad,
    to serve

1 Pour the hot chicken stock into a jug (pitcher). Stir in the saffron threads and set aside.

2 Heat the butter in a pan and fry the onion and garlic for 5 minutes. Add the cinnamon stick, cardamoms and bay leaf and cook for 2 minutes.

3 Drain the rice, add to the pan, then cook, stirring, for 2 minutes. Add the saffron stock and sultanas.

4 Bring to the boil, stir, then lower the heat, cover and cook gently for 10 minutes or until the rice is tender and all the liquid has been absorbed.

5 Meanwhile, heat the oil in a wok, karahi or large pan and fry the cashew nuts until browned. Drain the nuts on kitchen paper, then sprinkle the cashew nuts over the rice. Serve with naan bread and tomato and onion salad.

Nutritional information per portion: Energy 477kcal/2002kJ; Protein 8g; Carbohydrate 69g, of which sugars 11g; Fat 21g, of which saturates 8g; Cholesterol 27mg; Calcium 197mg; Fibre 2.7g; Sodium 380mg.

Mushroom pilau

This dish is simplicity itself. Serve with any Indian dish or with roast lamb or chicken. For a nuttier pilau, stir in a handful of toasted cashew nuts when the rice is ready.

SERVES 4

30ml/2 tbsp vegetable oil
2 shallots, finely chopped
1 garlic clove, crushed
3 green cardamom pods
25g/1oz/2 tbsp ghee or butter
175g/6oz/2¹/₂ cups button (white)
  mushrooms, sliced
225g/8oz/generous 1 cup basmati
  rice, soaked and drained
5ml/1 tsp grated fresh root ginger
good pinch of garam masala
450ml/³/₄ pint/scant 2 cups water
15ml/1 tbsp chopped fresh
  coriander (cilantro)
salt

1 Heat the vegetable oil in a flameproof casserole and fry the shallots, garlic and cardamom pods over medium heat for about 3–4 minutes, stirring frequently, until the shallots have softened and are beginning to brown.

2 Add the ghee or butter. When it has melted, add the mushrooms and fry for 2–3 minutes more.

3 Add the rice, ginger and garam masala. Cook over low heat for 2–3 minutes, stirring constantly, then stir in the water and a little salt. Bring to the boil, then cover tightly and simmer over very low heat for 10 minutes.

4 Remove the casserole from the heat. Leave to stand, covered, for 5 minutes. Add the chopped fresh coriander and fork it through the rice. Spoon the rice into a warmed serving bowl and serve immediately.

Nutritional information per portion: Energy 309kcal/1286kJ; Protein 5.2g; Carbohydrate 46.3g, of which sugars 1g; Fat 11.2g, of which saturates 4g; Cholesterol 13mg; Calcium 18mg; Fibre 0.7g; Sodium 41mg.

Creamy fish pilau

This salmon dish is fusion food at its most exciting – the method for the recipe comes from India but the creamy wine sauce has a French flavour.

SERVES 4–6

450g/1lb fresh mussels, scrubbed
350ml/12fl oz/1½ cups white wine
fresh flat leaf parsley sprig
about 675g/1½lb salmon
225g/8oz scallops
about 15ml/1 tbsp olive oil
40g/1½oz/3 tbsp butter
2 shallots, finely chopped
225g/8oz/3 cups button (white)
   mushrooms
275g/10oz/1½ cups basmati rice,
   soaked for 30 minutes and drained
300ml/½ pint/1¼ cups fish stock
150ml/¼ pint/²⁄₃ cup double
   (heavy) cream
15ml/1 tbsp chopped fresh parsley
225g/8oz large cooked prawns (shrimp),
   peeled and deveined
salt and ground black pepper
fresh flat leaf parsley sprigs, to garnish

1 Preheat the oven to 160°C/325°F/Gas 3. Place the mussels in a pan with 90ml/6 tbsp of the wine and the parsley. Cover and cook for 4–5 minutes until the mussels have opened. Drain, reserving the cooking liquid. Remove the mussels from their shells, discarding any that have not opened. Cut the salmon into bitesize pieces. Detach the corals from the scallops and cut the white flesh into thick, even pieces.

2 Heat half the oil and all the butter and fry the shallots and mushrooms for 3–4 minutes. Transfer to a bowl. Heat the remaining oil and fry the rice for about 2–3 minutes. Spoon into a flameproof casserole.

3 Pour the stock, remaining wine and reserved mussel liquid into a frying pan, and bring to the boil. Off the heat, stir in the cream and parsley. Season. Pour over the rice, then add the salmon and scallops, and the mushroom mixture. Cover and bake for 30–35 minutes, then add the scallop corals, and cook for 4 minutes. Add the mussels and prawns and cook for 3–4 minutes until heated through and the rice is tender. Serve garnished with the parsley.

Nutritional information per portion: Energy 428kcal/1787kJ; Protein 24.2g; Carbohydrate 39g, of which sugars 1.1g; Fat 15.2g, of which saturates 8.7g; Cholesterol 134mg; Calcium 130mg; Fibre 0.8g; Sodium 200mg.

Spiced fish with pumpkin rice

This is a dish of contrasts – the slightly sweet flavour of pumpkin, the mildly spicy fish, and the deliciously aromatic coriander and ginger mixture that is stirred in at the end – are all bound together with well-flavoured, tender rice.

SERVES 4

450g/1lb sea bass, skinned and boned
30ml/2 tbsp plain (all-purpose) flour
5ml/1 tsp ground coriander
1.5–2.5ml/¹⁄₄–¹⁄₂ tsp ground turmeric
500g/1¹⁄₄lb pumpkin flesh
30–45ml/2–3 tbsp olive oil
6 spring onions (scallions), sliced
1 garlic clove, finely chopped
275g/10oz/1¹⁄₂ cups basmati rice, soaked
550ml/18fl oz/2¹⁄₂ cups fish stock
salt and ground black pepper
lime or lemon wedges and fresh coriander
    (cilantro) sprigs, to serve

FOR THE FLAVOURING MIXTURE
45ml/3 tbsp finely chopped fresh
    coriander (cilantro)
10ml/2 tsp chopped fresh root ginger
¹⁄₂–1 fresh chilli, seeded and chopped
45ml/3 tbsp lime or lemon juice

1 Cut the fish into 2cm/³⁄₄in chunks. Mix the flour with the coriander, turmeric and a little salt and pepper and coat the fish. Set aside. Mix all the ingredients for the flavouring mixture.

2 Cut the pumpkin into 2cm/³⁄₄in chunks. Heat 15ml/1 tbsp oil in a flameproof casserole and stir-fry the spring onions and garlic for a few minutes until softened. Add the pumpkin to the pan and cook over a fairly low heat, stirring, for about 4–5 minutes.

3 Drain the rice, add to the pan and toss over a brisk heat for 2–3 minutes. Stir in the stock. Bring to simmering point, then lower the heat, cover and cook for 12–15 minutes.

4 Heat the remaining oil in a pan and fry the fish for 3 minutes on each side. Stir the flavouring mixture into the rice and transfer to a serving dish. Lay the fish on top. Serve with the coriander, and lemon or lime wedges to squeeze.

Nutritional information per portion: Energy 436kcal/1825kJ; Protein 27.9g; Carbohydrate 64.2g, of which sugars 3g; Fat 7.2g, of which saturates 1.1g; Cholesterol 52mg; Calcium 101mg; Fibre 2.3g; Sodium 73mg.

Prawn pilau

This pilau from Goa combines tasty prawns with a very simple preparation method. Although it perfectly delicious when served alone, the dish will also fit easily into a spread that includes meat, poultry and vegetable dishes.

SERVES 4

60ml/4 tbsp sunflower oil or olive oil
5cm/2in piece of cinnamon stick, halved
6 green cardamom pods, bruised
4 cloves
2 bay leaves, crumpled
1 large onion, finely sliced
10ml/2 tsp ginger purée
1 green chilli, finely chopped, and seeded
    if preferred
5ml/¹/₂ tsp ground turmeric
5ml/1 tsp salt, or to taste
15ml/1 tbsp chopped fresh
    coriander (cilantro)
250g/9oz cooked and peeled
    prawns (shrimp)
275g/10oz/1¹/₃ cups basmati rice,
    soaked and drained

1 In a heavy pan, heat the oil over a low heat and add the cinnamon, cardamom, cloves and bay leaves. Stir-fry the ingredients gently for 25–30 seconds and then add the onion. Increase the heat to medium, and fry until the onion is beginning to brown, around 7–8 minutes, stirring regularly to prevent the spices from burning.

2 Add the ginger purée and chilli to the pan and continue to fry until the onion is well browned.

3 Add the turmeric, salt, chopped coriander, prawns and rice to the pan. Stir gently to mix the ingredients. Stir-fry for about 2–3 minutes, then pour in 475ml/16fl oz/2 cups hot water. Bring the mixture to the boil and let it cook, uncovered, for 2–3 minutes. Reduce the heat to low, cover the pan tightly and cook for a further 7–8 minutes.

4 Remove from the heat and leave to stand for 5–6 minutes to absorb the flavour. Fluff up the pilau with a fork and transfer it to a serving dish.

Nutritional information per portion: Energy 440kcal/1835kJ; Protein 17.9g; Carbohydrate 64.1g, of which sugars 5.6g; Fat 12.4g, of which saturates 1.3g; Cholesterol 122mg; Calcium 94mg; Fibre 1.4g; Sodium 123mg.

Chicken pilau

This moist chicken curry has a long list of ingredients, but the final result is well worth the effort. Freshly ground spices and the addition of star anise provide a great taste experience.

SERVES 4

10ml/2 tsp coriander seeds
5ml/1 tsp cumin seeds
1–3 dried red chillies, chopped
10 black peppercorns
30ml/2 tbsp white poppy seeds
15ml/1 tbsp sesame seeds
45ml/3 tbsp sunflower or olive oil
1 medium onion, finely sliced
10ml/2 tsp ginger purée
10ml/2 tsp garlic purée
2.5ml/^{1}/$_{2}$ tsp ground turmeric
450g/1lb skinless chicken thigh
    fillets, halved

75g/3oz/^{1}/$_{3}$ cup thick set natural (plain)
    yogurt, whisked
5ml/1 tsp salt, or to taste
15ml/1 tbsp ghee or unsalted butter
2.5cm/1in piece of cinnamon stick
6 green cardamom pods, bruised
6 cloves
2 star anise
275g/10oz basmati rice, washed and soaked
    for 20 minutes, then drained
2.5ml/^{1}/$_{2}$ tsp salt, or to taste
15ml/1 tbsp toasted flaked (sliced) almonds,
    to garnish

1 Preheat a small heavy pan over a low heat and dry-fry the coriander and cumin seeds for 25–30 seconds. Add the chillies, peppercorns, poppy and sesame seeds for 25–30 seconds. Grind the ingredients in a food processor until fine, and set aside.

2 In a pan, heat the oil and fry the onion for 5 minutes. Add the ginger and garlic and fry for 3–4 minutes. Add the turmeric and chicken, and increase the heat slightly for 5 minutes. Add the yogurt and cook for 5 minutes, stirring. Add the ground spices and the salt, and cook for 3 minutes. Pour in 75ml/2^{1}/$_{2}$fl oz/^{1}/$_{3}$ cup warm water, cook for 5 minutes or until the liquid has evaporated.

3 In another pan, heat the ghee or butter and stir-fry the cinnamon stick, cardamom pods, cloves and star anise for about 2 minutes. Add the rice, salt and 475ml/16fl oz/2 cups water. Bring to the boil, then simmer, covered, for 7–8 minutes. Add the chicken. Leave to stand, covered, for 20 minutes. Mix the ingredients and serve garnished with almonds.

Nutritional information per portion: Energy 487kcal/2035kJ; Protein 25.2g; Carbohydrate 65.5g, of which sugars 11.3g; Fat 13.7g, of which saturates 1.8g; Cholesterol 89mg; Calcium 55mg; Fibre 2g; Sodium 829mg.

Spicy lamb and vegetable pilau

Tender lamb is served in this dish with basmati rice and a colourful selection of vegetables and cashew nuts. The dish is presented in cabbage leaf 'bowls'.

SERVES 4

450g/1lb boned shoulder of lamb, cubed
2.5ml/¹/₂ tsp dried thyme
2.5ml/¹/₂ tsp paprika
5ml/1 tsp garam masala
1 garlic clove, crushed
25ml/1¹/₂ tbsp vegetable oil
900ml/1¹/₂ pints/3³/₄ cups stock
large Savoy cabbage leaves, to serve

FOR THE RICE

25g/1oz/2 tbsp butter
1 onion, chopped
1 medium potato, diced

1 carrot, sliced
¹/₂ red (bell) pepper, chopped
1 green chilli, seeded and chopped
115g/4oz/1 cup sliced cabbage
60ml/4 tbsp natural (plain) yogurt
2.5ml/¹/₂ tsp ground cumin
5 green cardamom pods
2 garlic cloves, crushed
225g/8oz/generous 1 cup basmati rice,
    soaked and drained
50g/2oz/¹/₂ cup cashew nuts
salt and ground black pepper

1 Put the lamb cubes in a large bowl and add the thyme, paprika, garam masala and garlic, with plenty of salt and pepper. Stir, cover, and leave in a cool place for 2–3 hours.

2 Heat the oil in a pan and brown the lamb, in batches, over a medium heat for 5–6 minutes. Stir in the stock, cover, and cook for 35–40 minutes. Using a slotted spoon, transfer the lamb to a bowl. Pour the liquid into a measuring jug (cup), topping it up with water if necessary to make 600ml/1 pint/ 2¹/₂ cups.

3 For the rice, melt the butter in a separate pan and fry the onion, potato and carrot for about 5 minutes. Add the red pepper and chilli and fry for 3 minutes more, then stir in the cabbage, yogurt, spices, garlic and the reserved lamb stock. Stir well, cover, then simmer gently for 5–10 minutes, until the cabbage has wilted.

4 Stir the rice into the stew and add the lamb. Cover and simmer over a low heat for 20 minutes or until the rice is cooked. Sprinkle in the cashew nuts and season to taste with salt and pepper. Serve hot, cupped in cabbage leaves.

Nutritional information per portion: Energy 751kcal/3135kJ; Protein 33.7g; Carbohydrate 86.3g, of which sugars 7.3g; Fat 30.1g, of which saturates 11.6g; Cholesterol 102mg; Calcium 88mg; Fibre 2.3g; Sodium 200mg.

Chicken biryani

Easy to make and very tasty, this is a simple baked rice dish that would be ideal for a family supper. Serve with an onion and tomato salad on the side.

SERVES 4

10 green cardamom pods
275g/10oz/1¹⁄₂ cups basmati rice
2.5ml/¹⁄₂ tsp salt
2–3 cloves
5cm/2in cinnamon stick
45ml/3 tbsp vegetable oil
3 onions, sliced
4 skinless chicken breast fillets, cubed
1.5ml/¹⁄₄ tsp ground cloves
5ml/1 tsp each ground cumin and coriander
2.5ml/¹⁄₂ tsp ground black pepper
3 garlic cloves, chopped
5ml/1 tsp chopped fresh root ginger
juice of 1 lemon
4 tomatoes, sliced
30ml/2 tbsp chopped fresh coriander
  (cilantro), plus extra to garnish
150ml/¹⁄₄ pint/²⁄₃ cup natural (plain)
  yogurt, plus extra to serve
4–5 saffron threads, soaked in 10ml/
  2 tsp hot milk
toasted flaked (sliced) almonds,
  to garnish

1 Preheat the oven to 190°C/375°F/Gas 5. Remove the seeds from half the cardamom pods and grind them finely. Set aside.

2 Bring a flameproof casserole of water to the boil. Add the rice, then salt, the remaining whole cardamom pods, cloves and cinnamon stick. Boil the rice for 2 minutes, then drain, leaving the whole spices in the rice.

3 Heat the oil in the flameproof casserole and fry the onions for 8 minutes, until soft and browned.

4 Add the chicken, ground spices and the ground cardamom seeds. Mix, then add the garlic, ginger and lemon juice. Stir-fry for 5 minutes.

5 Arrange the sliced tomatoes on top. Sprinkle with the coriander, spoon over the yogurt, and top with the rice.

6 Drizzle the saffron milk over the rice and add 150ml/¹⁄₄ pint/²⁄₃ cup water. Cover and bake for 1 hour. Garnish with the almonds and coriander and serve with the yogurt.

Nutritional information per portion: Energy 563kcal/2359kJ; Protein 45.4g; Carbohydrate 70g, of which sugars 12.5g; Fat 11.3g, of which saturates 1.7g; Cholesterol 105mg; Calcium 152mg; Fibre 3.2g; Sodium 138mg.

Lamb biryani

This is a traditional festive, one-pot dish of baked rice, layered with lamb, with crispy fried onion sprinkled on top. It can be served hot and the leftovers eaten the next day.

SERVES 4–5

675g/1¹/₂lb leg of lamb, cubed
50g/2oz/¹/₄ cup natural (plain) yogurt
5ml/1 tsp salt
75g/3oz ghee
2 large onions, finely sliced
10ml/2 tsp each ginger and garlic purée

FOR THE GROUND SPICE MIX

10ml/2 tsp coriander seeds, ground
5ml/1 tsp cumin seeds, ground
2.5cm/1in cinnamon stick, ground
4 each cardamoms and cloves, ground
15ml/1 tbsp poppy seeds, ground
¹/₄ of a whole nutmeg, grated

FOR THE RICE

2.5ml/¹/₂ tsp saffron, pounded
30ml/2 tbsp hot milk
350g/12oz/1³/₄ cups basmati rice
2.5cm/1in cinnamon stick
4 each cardamoms and cloves, bruised
2 each star anise and bay leaves
10ml/2 tsp salt, or to taste
15ml/1 tbsp ghee, melted

1 Put the lamb in a large bowl. Add the yogurt and salt. Mix, and set aside for 20–30 minutes.

2 Melt the ghee and fry the onions. Drain on kitchen paper. Return the pan to the heat and add the ginger and garlic, and fry for 1 minute. Add the ground spice mix and stir-fry for 1–2 minutes. Add the lamb. Stir and cook over a medium heat for 2–3 minutes, then remove from the heat.

3 For the rice, soak the saffron in the hot milk and set aside. Preheat the oven to 160°C/ 325°F/Gas Mark 3. Wash and drain the rice, then parboil for 5 minutes in 1.5 litres/2¹/₂ pints/6¹/₄ cups water. Add the remaining ingredients except the ghee. Boil for 3 minutes, drain and reserve the spices.

4 Spread the lamb evenly in a heavy, ovenproof pan. Top with half the fried onions and pile the rice on top, with the whole spices. Sprinkle the saffron milk and melted ghee over the top.

5 Seal the pan with a double thickness of foil and cover with the lid. Cook in the oven for 1 hour. Leave to stand for 30 minutes. Stir with a metal spoon to mix the rice and meat. Transfer to a serving dish and garnish with fried onions.

Nutritional information per portion: Energy 769kcal/3208kJ; Protein 43.6g; Carbohydrate 67.6g, of which sugars 14.5g; Fat 36.2g, of which saturates 15g; Cholesterol 142mg; Calcium 134mg; Fibre 2.6g; Sodium 252mg.

Beef biryani

Moguls brought this spicy dry curry to central India. Encased in rice and spices and baked in the oven, the beef becomes deliciously tender and tasty.

SERVES 4

2 large onions
2 garlic cloves, chopped
2.5cm/1in root ginger, chopped
1 green chilli, seeded and chopped
bunch of fresh coriander (cilantro)
60ml/4 tbsp flaked (sliced) almonds
30–45ml/2–3 tbsp water
15ml/1 tbsp butter, plus 30ml/2 tbsp butter,
  for the rice
45ml/3 tbsp sunflower oil
30ml/2 tbsp sultanas (golden raisins)

500g/1¼lb braising steak, cubed
5ml/1 tsp ground coriander
15ml/1 tbsp ground cumin
2.5ml/½ tsp ground turmeric
2.5ml/½ tsp ground fenugreek
good pinch of ground cinnamon
175ml/6fl oz/¾ cup natural (plain) yogurt
275g/10oz/1½ cups basmati rice
1.2 litres/2 pints/5 cups stock
salt and ground black pepper
2 hard-boiled eggs, chopped, to garnish

1 Chop 1 onion. Place in a food processor with the garlic, ginger, chilli, coriander, half the almonds and water and process to a paste. Slice the remaining onion into rings. Heat half the butter and oil in a flameproof casserole and fry the onion for 10–15 minutes. Transfer to a plate. Fry the rest of the almonds and set aside, then fry the sultanas until they swell. Transfer to the plate.

2 Heat the remaining butter in the casserole with 15ml/1 tbsp of the oil. Fry the meat, in batches, until brown and set aside. Heat the remaining oil and pour in the spice paste. Stir-fry for 2–3 minutes. Stir in all the spices, season and cook for 1 minute. Lower the heat, then stir in the yogurt and the meat. Stir to coat, cover tightly and simmer for 45 minutes until the meat is tender.

3 Soak the rice in a bowl of cold water for 15 minutes. Preheat the oven to 160°C/325°F/Gas 3. Drain the rice, place in a pan and add the stock. Bring to the boil, cover and cook for 6 minutes. Drain the rice and mound on top of the meat in the casserole. Using a spoon handle, make a hole through the rice and meat mixture, to the bottom. Sprinkle with fried onions, almonds and sultanas and dot with butter. Cover with a lid. Cook in the oven for 30–40 minutes. To serve, place on a warmed serving plate and garnish with the eggs. Serve immediately.

Nutritional information per portion: Energy 778kcal/3240kJ; Protein 40g; Carbohydrate 70.4g, of which sugars 13.4g; Fat 37.4g, of which saturates 11.8g; Cholesterol 94mg; Calcium 164mg; Fibre 2.3g; Sodium 183mg.

Kedgeree

This classic dish is best made with basmati rice, which goes well with the mild curry flavour, but other long grain rice will do. For a colourful garnish, add some finely sliced red onion and a little red onion marmalade.

SERVES 4

450g/1lb undyed smoked haddock fillet
750ml/1¼ pints/3 cups milk
2 bay leaves
¹/₂ lemon, sliced
50g/2oz/¼ cup butter
1 onion, chopped
2.5ml/¹/₂ tsp ground turmeric
5ml/1 tsp mild curry powder
2 green cardamom pods
350g/12oz/1³/₄ cups basmati or long grain rice, washed and drained
4 hard-boiled eggs, coarsely chopped
150ml/¼ pint/²/₃ cup single (light) cream (optional)
30ml/2 tbsp chopped fresh parsley, to garnish
salt and ground black pepper

1 Put the haddock in a pan and add the milk, bay leaves and lemon slices. Poach gently for 8–10 minutes, until the haddock flakes easily. Strain the milk into a jug (pitcher), discarding the bay leaves and lemon slices. Remove the skin from the haddock and flake the flesh into large pieces. Keep hot until required.

2 Melt the butter in the pan, add the onion and cook over a low heat for about 3 minutes, until softened. Stir in the turmeric, the curry powder and cardamom pods and cook for 1 minute.

3 Add the rice, stirring to coat it with the butter. Add the reserved milk, stir and bring to the boil. Lower the heat and simmer the rice for 10–12 minutes, until all the milk has been absorbed and the rice is tender. Season to taste.

4 Gently stir in the fish and hard-boiled eggs, with the cream, if using. Sprinkle with the parsley and serve.

Nutritional information per portion: Energy 320kcal/1336kJ; Protein 15.6g; Carbohydrate 46.6g, of which sugars 0g; Fat 7.6g, of which saturates 3.3g; Cholesterol 149mg; Calcium 39mg; Fibre 0g; Sodium 357mg.

Vegetarian kedgeree

This spicy lentil and rice dish is a delicious variation of the original Indian version of kedgeree, known as kitchiri. You can serve it as it is, or topped with quartered hard-boiled eggs. It is also good with grilled mushrooms.

SERVES 4

50g/2oz/¼ cup red split lentils, rinsed
1 bay leaf
225g/8oz/1 cup basmati rice, rinsed
    and drained
4 cloves
50g/2oz/4 tbsp butter
5ml/1 tsp curry powder
2.5ml/½ tsp mild chilli powder
30ml/2 tbsp chopped fresh flat
    leaf parsley
salt and ground black pepper
4 hard-boiled eggs, quartered, to
    serve (optional)

1 Put the lentils in a pan, add the bay leaf and cover with cold water. Bring to the boil, skim off any foam, then reduce the heat. Cover and simmer for 25–30 minutes, until tender. Drain, then discard the bay leaf.

2 Meanwhile, place the rice in a pan and cover with about 475ml/16fl oz/ 2 cups boiling water. Add the cloves and a pinch of salt. Cook, covered, for 10–15 minutes, until all the water is absorbed and the rice is tender. Discard the cloves.

3 Melt the butter over a gentle heat in a large frying pan, then add the curry and chilli powders and cook for 1 minute.

4 Stir the lentils and rice into the pan and mix well until they are coated in the spiced butter. Season and cook for 1–2 minutes until heated through. Stir in the parsley and serve immediately with the hard-boiled eggs, if using.

Nutritional information per portion: Energy 481kcal/2015kJ; Protein 14.8g; Carbohydrate 72.6g, of which sugars 4.1g; Fat 15.2g, of which saturates 3.5g; Cholesterol 0mg; Calcium 65mg; Fibre 2.8g; Sodium 82mg.

Breads

There are myriad recipes for breads such as the simple traditional flat bread, which can be embellished with spices and vegetables. Richer variations include ghee or butter and milk to make flaky confections such as parathas, or deep-fried, puffy pooris or bhaturas. The bread most of us are familiar with is naan, which is made here with a mixture of spicy aromatic seeds, or with the addition of garlic and coriander.

Deep-fried soft puffed bread

Kumol Lusi are made with plain flour and the dough is enriched with ghee and hot milk, creating a velvety soft bread. They are perfect with any vegetable curry or spiced omelettes. A healthier version can be made by using wholemeal flour and adding olive oil instead of ghee. This creates a wholesome taste that complements most vegetable curries, lentils, beans and peas.

MAKES 16

275g/10oz/2¹/₂ cups plain (all-purpose)
  flour, plus a little extra for dusting
2.5ml/¹/₂ tsp salt
1.5ml/¹/₄ tsp sugar

15ml/1 tbsp ghee or unsalted (sweet) butter
175ml/6fl oz /²/₃ cup lukewarm milk
oil for deep frying

1 Sift the flour into a large bowl and add the salt, sugar and ghee or butter. Mix the ingredients well and gradually add the milk. Mix until a soft dough is formed, then transfer it to a flat surface. Knead for 4–5 minutes. Alternatively, make the dough in a food processor. Wrap the dough in clear film (plastic wrap) and let it rest for 20–30 minutes.

2 Divide the dough into 2 equal parts and make 8 equal-sized balls out of each. Flatten the balls into cakes by rotating and pressing them between your palms.

3 Dust each cake very lightly in the flour and roll them out to about 6cm/2¹/₂in circles, taking care not to tear or pierce them, as they will not puff up if damaged. Place them in a single layer on a piece of baking parchment and cover with another piece.

4 Heat the oil in a wok or other suitable pan for deep-frying, over a medium/high heat. When the oil has a faint shimmer of rising smoke on the surface, carefully drop in one dough cake and as soon as it floats, gently tap round the edges to encourage puffing. When it has puffed up, turn it over and fry the other side until browned.

5 Drain on kitchen paper. Keep the fried breads on a tray in a single layer. They are best eaten fresh, although they can be reheated briefly (3–4 minutes) in a moderately hot oven. Serve with Egg, Potato and Green Pea Curry.

Nutritional information per portion: Energy 72kcal/306kJ; Protein 2g; Carbohydrate 14g, of which sugars 0.9g; Fat 1.3g, of which saturates 0.6g; Cholesterol 1mg; Calcium 37mg; Fibre 0.5g; Sodium 68mg.

Pooris

These delicious little deep-fried breads, shaped into discs, make it very easy to overindulge. If you wish, spinach with fresh root ginger and ground cumin can be added to the dough.

MAKES 12

115g/4oz/1 cup unbleached plain (all-purpose) flour

115g/4oz/1 cup wholemeal (whole-wheat) flour

2.5ml/½ tsp salt

2.5ml/½ tsp chilli powder

30ml/2 tbsp vegetable oil

100–120ml/3½–4fl oz/scant ⅓ – ½ cup water

vegetable oil, for frying

1 Sift the flours, salt and chilli powder into a mixing bowl. Add the vegetable oil then add sufficient water to mix to a dough. Turn out on to a lightly floured surface and knead for 8–10 minutes until smooth. Place in an oiled bowl and cover with oiled clear film (plastic wrap). Leave for 30 minutes.

2 Turn out on to the floured surface. Divide the dough into 12 equal pieces. Keeping the rest of the dough covered, roll one piece into a 13cm/5in round. Repeat with the remaining dough. Stack the pooris, layered between sheets of lightly oiled clear film, to keep them moist.

3 Pour the oil for frying to a depth of 2.5cm/1in in a deep frying pan and heat it to 180°C/350°F. Gently slide one poori into the oil; it will sink but will return to the surface and begin to sizzle. Gently press the poori into the oil. It will puff up. Turn the poori over after a few seconds and allow it to cook for a further 20–30 seconds. Remove the poori from the pan and pat dry with kitchen paper then place it on a large baking tray, in a single layer, and keep warm in a low oven while you cook the remaining pooris. Serve while warm.

Nutritional information per portion: Energy 120kcal/501kJ; Protein 2.1g; Carbohydrate 13.5g, of which sugars 0.3g; Fat 6.7g, of which saturates 0.8g; Cholesterol 0mg; Calcium 17mg; Fibre 1.2g; Sodium 164mg.

Bhaturas

These leavened and deep-fried breads are from Punjab, where the local people enjoy them with a bowl of chickpea curry. Bhaturas are soft and fluffy, with a pleasant chewy texture.

MAKES 10

15g/¹/₂oz fresh yeast
5ml/1 tsp sugar
120ml/4fl oz/¹/₂ cup lukewarm water
200g/7oz/1³/₄ cups plain
   (all-purpose) flour
50g/2oz/¹/₂ cup semolina
2.5ml/¹/₂ tsp salt
15g/¹/₂oz/1 tbsp ghee or butter
30ml/2 tbsp natural (plain) yogurt
vegetable oil, for frying

1 Mix the yeast with the sugar and water in a jug (pitcher). Sift the flour into a mixing bowl and add the semolina and salt. Rub in the ghee or butter. Add the yeast mixture and yogurt to the bowl and mix to a dough. Turn out on to a lightly floured surface and knead for about 10 minutes until smooth and elastic.

2 Place the dough in an oiled bowl, cover with oiled clear film (plastic wrap) and leave to rise, in a warm place, for about 1 hour, or until doubled in size. Turn out on to a lightly floured surface and knock back (punch down). Divide into ten equal pieces and shape each into a ball. Flatten into discs with the palm of your hand. Roll out on a lightly floured surface into 13cm/5in rounds.

3 Heat oil to a depth of 1cm/¹/₂in in a deep frying pan and slide in one bhatura. Fry for 1 minute, turning over after 30 seconds, then drain on kitchen paper. Keep warm in a low oven while frying the remaining bhaturas. Serve immediately, while hot.

Nutritional information per portion: Energy 141kcal/590kJ; Protein 2.6g; Carbohydrate 19.7g, of which sugars 0.5g; Fat 6.3g, of which saturates 1.3g; Cholesterol 0mg; Calcium 35mg; Fibre 0.7g; Sodium 102mg.

Missi rotis

These delicious unleavened breads are a speciality from Punjab in India. Gram flour, also known as besan, is made from ground chickpeas and is combined here with the traditional wheat flour.

MAKES 4

115g/4oz/1 cup gram flour

115g/4oz/1 cup wholemeal (whole-wheat) flour

1 fresh green chilli, seeded and chopped

1/2 onion, finely chopped

15ml/1 tbsp chopped fresh coriander (cilantro)

2.5ml/1/2 tsp ground turmeric

2.5ml/1/2 tsp salt

15ml/1 tbsp vegetable oil or melted butter

120–150ml/4–5fl oz/1/2– 2/3 cup lukewarm water

30–45ml/2–3 tbsp melted unsalted butter or ghee

1 Mix the two types of flour, chilli, onion, coriander, turmeric and salt together in a large mixing bowl. Stir in the 15ml/1 tbsp vegetable oil or melted butter. Mix sufficient water into the mixture to make a pliable soft dough. Turn out the dough on to a lightly floured surface and knead with your hands until smooth. Place in a lightly oiled bowl, cover with lightly oiled clear film (plastic wrap) and leave to rest for 30 minutes.

2 Turn the dough out on to a lightly floured surface. Divide the dough into four equal pieces and shape into balls in the palms of your hands. Roll out each ball into a thick round about 15–18cm/6–7in in diameter.

3 Heat a griddle or heavy frying pan over medium heat for a few minutes until hot. Brush both sides of one roti with some melted butter or ghee. Add it to the griddle or frying pan and cook for about 2 minutes, turning after 1 minute. Brush the cooked roti lightly with melted butter or ghee again, slide it on to a plate and keep warm in a low oven while cooking the remaining rotis in the same way. Serve the rotis immediately while still warm.

Nutritional information per portion: Energy 298kcal/1267kJ; Protein 8.5g; Carbohydrate 65.8g, of which sugars 1.6g; Fat 2g, of which saturates 0.3g; Cholesterol 0mg; Calcium 114mg; Fibre 3.2g; Sodium 3mg.

Tandoori rotis

Roti means bread, and it is the most common food in central and northern India. Roti is basically made with just wholemeal flour, salt and water, with the addition of a little fat.

MAKES 6

350g/12oz/3 cups chapati flour or wholemeal (whole-wheat) flour
5ml/1 tsp salt
250ml/8fl oz/1 cup water
30–45ml/2–3 tbsp melted ghee or unsalted butter, for brushing

1 Sift the flour and salt into a mixing bowl. Add the water to the bowl and mix it with your hands or a wooden spoon until a soft, pliable dough forms.

2 Knead the dough on a lightly floured work surface for about 3–4 minutes until smooth. Place it in a lightly oiled bowl, cover with lightly oiled clear film (plastic wrap) and leave to rest for 1 hour.

3 Turn out the dough on to a lightly floured surface. Divide the dough into six even pieces and shape each into a ball with your hands. Press each out into a larger round with the palm of your hand, cover with a piece of lightly oiled clear film and leave to rest for about 10 minutes.

4 Meanwhile, preheat the oven to 230°C/450°F/Gas 8. Place three baking sheets in the oven to heat.

5 Roll the rotis into 15cm/6in rounds, place two on each baking sheet and bake for 8–10 minutes. Brush with melted ghee or butter and serve warm.

Nutritional information per portion: Energy 244kcal/1030kJ; Protein 5.5g; Carbohydrate 45.3g, of which sugars 0.9g; Fat 5.8g, of which saturates 2.5g; Cholesterol 0mg; Calcium 82mg; Fibre 1.8g; Sodium 329mg.

Red lentil pancakes

This is a type of dosa, which is essentially a pancake from southern India, but it is used in a similar fashion to north Indian bread.

MAKES 6

150g/5oz/³/₄ cup long grain rice
50g/2oz/¹/₄ cup red split lentils
250ml/8fl oz/1 cup warm water
5ml/1 tsp salt
2.5ml/¹/₂ tsp ground turmeric
2.5ml/¹/₂ tsp ground black pepper
30ml/2 tbsp chopped fresh coriander
   (cilantro)
vegetable oil, for frying and drizzling

1 Place the rice and lentils in a large bowl, cover with the warm water, cover and soak for at least 8 hours or overnight. Drain off the water and reserve. Place the rice and lentils in a food processor or blender and blend until smooth. Blend in the reserved soaking water. Scrape into a bowl, cover with clear film (plastic wrap) and leave in a warm place to ferment for 24 hours.

2 Stir the salt, turmeric, black pepper and coriander into the rice mixture. Heat a frying pan over medium heat for a few minutes until hot. Smear the pan with oil and add about 30–45ml/2–3 tbsp of the batter mixture.

3 Using the base of a soup spoon, gently spread the batter out, using a circular motion, to make a pancake that is about 15cm/6in in diameter.

4 Cook in the pan for 1¹/₂–2 minutes, or until set. Drizzle a little oil over the pancake and around the edges. Turn over and cook for about 1 minute, or until golden brown. Keep the pancakes warm in a low oven or on a plate over simmering water while cooking the remaining pancakes. Serve warm.

Nutritional information per portion: Energy 153kcal/641kJ; Protein 4.1g; Carbohydrate 25.1g, of which sugars 0.3g; Fat 4.1g, of which saturates 0.4g; Cholesterol 0mg; Calcium 21mg; Fibre 0.7g; Sodium 333mg.

Parathas

Making paratha is similar to making flaky pastry, although paratha can be handled freely, unlike flaky pastry. They can be plain or stuffed with onions or paneer, an Indian cheese.

MAKES 12–15

350g/12oz/3 cups chapati flour or an
    equal quantity of wholemeal
    (whole-wheat) flour and plain
    (all-purpose) flour
50g/2oz/¹/₂ cup plain (all-purpose) flour
    for dusting work surfaces
50g/2oz/¹/₂ cup plain (all-purpose) flour
5ml/1 tsp salt
40g/1¹/₂oz/3 tbsp ghee or unsalted
    butter

1 Sift the flours and salt into a bowl. Make a well in the centre and add 10ml/2 tsp melted ghee or butter. Fold it into the flour to make a crumbly texture. Gradually add water to the flour and ghee or butter in the bowl to make a soft, pliable dough. Knead until the dough is smooth. Cover and leave to rest for 30 minutes.

2 Melt the remaining ghee or butter in a small heavy pan over low heat. Divide the dough into about 12–15 equal portions and keep covered. Roll out each on a lightly floured surface to about 10cm/4in in diameter.

3 Brush the dough with a little of the melted ghee or butter and sprinkle with flour. With a sharp knife, make a straight cut from the centre to the edge of the dough, then lift a cut edge and roll the dough into a cone shape. Lift it and flatten it again into a ball.

4 Roll the dough out again on a lightly floured surface until it is about 18cm/7in wide. Heat a griddle and cook one paratha at a time, placing a little ghee along the edges. Cook on each side until golden. Serve hot.

Nutritional information per portion: Energy 108kcal/456kJ; Protein 2.3g; Carbohydrate 19.2g, of which sugars 0.4g; Fat 3g, of which saturates 1.3g; Cholesterol 0mg; Calcium 35mg; Fibre 0.8g; Sodium 132mg.

Spiced naan

Another excellent recipe for naan bread, this time it features aromatic fennel seeds, onion seeds and cumin seeds. Naan is quick and easy to make and can be made ahead if required.

MAKES 6

450g/1lb/4 cups strong white bread flour
5ml/1 tsp baking powder
2.5ml/¹/₂ tsp salt
1 sachet easy-blend (rapid-rise)
    dried yeast
5ml/1 tsp caster (superfine) sugar
5ml/1 tsp fennel seeds
10ml/2 tsp onion seeds
5ml/1 tsp cumin seeds
150ml/¹/₄ pint/²/₃ cup hand-hot milk
30ml/2 tbsp vegetable oil, plus extra
    for brushing
150ml/¹/₄ pint/²/₃ cup natural
    (plain) yogurt
1 egg, beaten

1 Sift the flour, baking powder and salt into a mixing bowl. Stir in the yeast, sugar, and all the seeds. Make a well in the centre. Stir the milk into the flour mixture, then add the oil, yogurt and egg. Mix to form a ball of dough.

2 Transfer the dough to a floured surface and knead for 10 minutes until smooth. Return to the clean, lightly oiled bowl and roll the dough to coat it with oil. Cover the bowl with clear film (plastic wrap) and set aside in a warm place until the dough has doubled in bulk.

3 Put a heavy baking sheet in the oven and preheat the oven to 240°C/475°F/Gas 9. Also preheat the grill (broiler). Knead the dough again lightly and divide it into six pieces. Keep five pieces covered while working with the sixth. Quickly roll the piece of dough out to a teardrop shape, brush lightly with oil and slap the naan on to the baking sheet.

4 Repeat with the remaining dough. Bake in the oven for 3 minutes or until puffed up, then place under the grill for about 30 seconds. Serve hot or warm.

Nutritional information per portion: Energy 311kcal/1319kJ; Protein 11g; Carbohydrate 63.8g, of which sugars 4.9g; Fat 3.2g, of which saturates 0.9g; Cholesterol 34mg; Calcium 197mg; Fibre 2.3g; Sodium 211mg.

Garlic and coriander naan

Traditionally cooked in a very hot clay oven known as a tandoor, naan is a leavened flatbread that is usually eaten with dry meat or vegetable curries.

MAKES 3

275g/10oz/2¹/₂ cups unbleached strong
   white bread flour
5ml/1 tsp salt
5ml/1 tsp dried yeast
60ml/4 tbsp natural (plain) yogurt
15ml/1 tbsp melted butter or ghee, plus
   30–45ml/2–3 tbsp for brushing
1 garlic clove, finely chopped
5ml/1 tsp black onion seeds
15ml/1 tbsp chopped fresh
   coriander (cilantro)
10ml/2 tsp clear honey, warmed

1 Sift the flour and salt into a large bowl. In a smaller bowl, cream the yeast with the yogurt. Set aside for 15 minutes. Add the yeast mixture to the flour with the smaller quantity of melted butter or ghee, and add the chopped garlic, black onion seeds and chopped coriander, mixing to a soft dough.

2 Transfer the dough to a floured surface and knead for 10 minutes. Place in a lightly oiled bowl, cover with lightly oiled clear film (plastic wrap) and leave to rise in a warm place for 45 minutes, or until doubled in bulk.

3 Preheat the oven to 230°C/450°F/Gas 8. Place three heavy baking sheets in the oven. On a lightly floured surface knock back (punch down) the dough. Divide into three and shape each into a ball. Cover two with oiled clear film and roll out the third into a teardrop shape.

4 Preheat the grill (broiler) to its highest setting. Place the naan on a hot baking sheet and bake for about 3–4 minutes, until puffed up. Remove from the oven, brush with honey and grill until browned slightly. Keep warm then make the remaining naan. Brush with melted butter or ghee and serve warm.

Nutritional information per portion: Energy 374kcal/1585kJ; Protein 10.4g; Carbohydrate 74.2g, of which sugars 2.9g; Fat 6.1g, of which saturates 3g; Cholesterol 11mg; Calcium 176mg; Fibre 2.8g; Sodium 706mg.

Tandoori leavened bread

This basic recipe for naan can be varied by adding your own toppings such as seeds, herbs and chillies. The perfect accompaniment for Indian curries, they also make a filling snack.

SERVES 4

500g/1¼lb/4½ cups self-raising (self-rising) flour
5ml/1 tsp baking powder
5ml/1 tsp salt
10ml/2 tsp sugar
50g/2oz/4 tbsp softened butter
250ml/8fl oz/1 cup warm milk
melted butter, to glaze

1 Sift the flour and add baking powder, salt and sugar. Mix, then rub in the butter. Gradually add the milk and mix until a dough is formed. Transfer to a pastry board and knead for 5 minutes. Cover with a damp cloth and leave for 30 minutes.

2 Preheat the grill (broiler) to high for 8–10 minutes, then line a grill (broiling) pan with a piece of foil and brush with a little oil. Divide the dough into eight equal-sized balls and flatten into cakes. Roll each into a circle 13cm/5in in diameter. Form into a teardrop shape.

3 Roll out again, in the teardrop shape. Place a naan in the grill pan and cook it for 1½ minutes until it puffs up. Keep checking as it can burn easily when it puffs up. Turn it and grill for 1 minute until brown patches appear. Place the cooked naan on a clean towel and brush the surface with a little melted butter.

4 Wrap the cooked naan in the towel to keep hot while you repeat the steps with the remaining dough and cook the other naans. Serve the bread with any meat, poultry or a vegetable curry dish.

Nutritional information per portion: Energy 630kcal/2666kJ; Protein 18.7g; Carbohydrate 117g, of which sugars 2.95g; Fat 13g, of which saturates 2.2g; Cholesterol 127mg; Calcium 246mg; Fibre 4.6g; Sodium 712mg.

Wholemeal flat bread

These breads are griddle-cooked, with oil or ghee spread over the surface. Unlike the dough for chapatis, this mixture contains a little fat and warm water is used instead of cold.

MAKES 8

400g/14oz/3¹/₂ cups chapati flour (atta) or fine wholemeal (whole-wheat) flour
5ml/1 tsp salt
30ml/2 tbsp sunflower oil or plain olive oil
250ml/9fl oz/1 cup lukewarm water
A little extra flour for dusting
Sunflower oil or plain olive oil for frying

1 Mix the flour and salt in a mixing bowl. Add the oil and work well into the flour with your fingertips. Gradually add the water and mix to a dough. Transfer it to a board and knead it for 4–5 minutes.

2 When all the excess moisture is absorbed by the flour, wrap the dough in clear film (plastic wrap) and let it rest for 30 minutes. Divide the dough into 8 balls and make flat cakes by rotating them between the palms and pressing them down. Roll out each cake on a floured surface into a 13cm/5in circle.

3 Pre-heat a heavy cast-iron or other similar griddle over a medium heat and place a rolled disc on it. Allow to cook for 2 minutes, then turn it over. Spread 5ml/1 tsp oil evenly on the surface and turn it over again. Cook for 2 minutes until browned all over. Spread 5ml/1 tsp oil on the second side, turn the bread over, and cook as above until browned.

4 Keep the breads hot by wrapping them in foil lined with kitchen paper or a clean dish towel. Cook the remaining flat breads in the same way. Serve with any curry.

Nutritional information per portion: Energy 180kcal/761kJ; Protein 6.4g; Carbohydrate 32g, of which sugars 1.1g; Fat 3.9g, of which saturates 0.5g; Cholesterol 0mg; Calcium 19mg; Fibre 4.5g; Sodium 247mg.

Spiced gram flour flat bread

For this bread, gram flour is kneaded together with grated onion, asafoetida and chillies. The bread is then griddle-roasted, which gives a delicious toasted aroma and a nutty taste. You can spread a little butter on the surface of the cooked bread to give it a more moist texture.

MAKES 8

400g/14oz/3½ cups gram flour, sifted
5ml/1 tsp nigella seeds
1.5ml/¼ tsp asafoetida
5ml/1 tsp salt or to taste
1 medium onion, grated
1 green chilli, finely chopped (seeded
    if you like)
45ml/3 tbsp coriander (cilantro) leaves,
    finely chopped
Gram flour for dusting
Oil for cooking

1 Put the gram flour in a mixing bowl and add the nigella seeds, asafoetida and salt. Mix well, then add the onion, green chilli and chopped coriander and mix until all the ingredients are well blended. Gradually add 100ml/ 3½ fl oz/7 tbsp water until a dough forms.

2 Transfer the dough to a flat surface and knead it for a couple of minutes with gentle pressure, turning it around frequently. If the dough sticks to your fingers, add a little oil. Divide the dough into 8 equal portions and flatten them into round cakes. Dust each cake in the flour and roll them out to circles of about 13cm/5in diameter.

3 Preheat a griddle over a low/medium heat and place a flat bread on it. Cook it for about a minute and then spread 15ml/1 tbsp oil around the edges. Continue to cook for a further 30–40 seconds or until browned. Turn the bread over and cook the second side until browned.

Nutritional information per portion: Energy 237kcal/1002kJ; Protein 4.5g; Carbohydrate 39.2g, of which sugars 0.4g; Fat 8.1g, of which saturates 0.9g; Cholesterol 0mg; Calcium 21mg; Fibre 6g; Sodium 1mg.

Punjabi cornmeal bread

This tasty bread is the mainstay of cooking in the Punjab and is simple to make. It is made using fine cornmeal, available from Indian grocers and health food stores. Alternatively, you can substitute polenta, which is widely available from supermarkets.

MAKES 8

175g/6oz/1¹/₂ cups cornmeal
90g/3¹/₂oz/³/₄ cup plain (all-purpose) flour
2.5ml/¹/₂ tsp salt
butter, to serve

1 Mix the cornmeal, flour and salt together. Gradually add 250–300ml/ 8–10fl oz/1–1¹/₄ cups warm water and mix until it forms a moist but firm dough, then transfer to a pastry board. Knead until it is soft and pliable. Cover the dough with a damp cloth and let it rest for 30 minutes. Meanwhile, preheat a cast-iron griddle or frying pan over a medium heat.

2 Divide the dough into eight equal-sized balls. Roll each between the palms, then flatten into a round cake 13cm/5in in diameter, patting with your fingertips. You can place the cakes between layers of clear film (plastic wrap) before cooking.

3 Lift a cake gently from the film and place on the heated griddle. Cook for 1 minute and turn over with a thin spatula. When the bread has set, cook both sides until brown patches appear. Remove from the griddle and spread butter on one side.

Nutritional information per portion: Energy 119kcal/500kJ; Protein 3.1g; Carbohydrate 24.7g, of which sugars 0.2g; Fat 0.9g, of which saturates 0g; Cholesterol 0mg; Calcium 17mg; Fibre 0.8g; Sodium 123mg.

Wheat-flour flat bread with spiced greens

In the state of Bihar, situated near west Bengal, this fabulous spicy wheat-flour flat bread is made with locally grown greens that are difficult to get hold of anywhere else. However, you can use spinach, which makes an easy and delicious alternative. This healthy flat bread is very tasty and is the perfect accompaniment to many Indian vegetarian dishes.

MAKES 10

250g/9oz spinach leaves
450g/1lb/4 cups chapati flour (atta) or fine
   wholemeal (whole-wheat) flour
5ml/1 tsp salt

2.5ml/¹/₂ tsp aniseeds
30ml/2 tbsp sunflower oil or plain olive oil
A little flour for dusting
Extra oil for shallow frying

1 Put the spinach in a large bowl or pan and pour over boiling water to cover it completely. Leave it to soak for 2 minutes, then drain, refresh with cold water and drain again. Squeeze out as much water as possible, but make sure that the spinach remains quite moist. Place the spinach in a food processor and chop it finely, but do not process it to a purée.

2 In a large mixing bowl, mix the flour, salt and aniseeds. Add 15ml/1 tbsp of the oil and mix well. Now, stir in the spinach, and gradually add 200ml/7fl oz/³/₄ cup water and mix until a soft dough is formed. You may not need all the water since the spinach leaves will release their own moisture into the flour, so add a little at a time.

3 Transfer to a flat surface, add the remaining oil and knead the dough for 3–4 minutes. Cover with a damp cloth and let it rest for 15–20 minutes.

4 Divide the dough into 2 equal parts and pinch off or cut each half into 5 equal portions. Form into balls and flatten each one into a smooth, round cake. Dust each cake in the flour and roll out each to approximately an 18cm/7in circle.

5 Pre-heat a griddle over a medium heat and place a flat bread on it. Cook for 30–40 seconds and turn it over. Spread 5ml/1 tsp of oil on the surface of the bread and turn it over again. Cook until brown patches appear underneath, checking by lifting the bread with a thin spatula or a fish slice. Spread 5ml/1 tsp oil on the second side, turn it over and cook until brown patches appear. Keep the breads hot by wrapping them in a piece of foil lined with kitchen paper until they are all cooked.

Nutritional information per portion: Energy 166kcal/700kJ; Protein 6.4g; Carbohydrate 29.2g, of which sugars 1.3g; Fat 3.4g, of which saturates 0.4g; Cholesterol 0mg; Calcium 60mg; Fibre 4.6g; Sodium 36mg.

Chutneys and Relishes

Nothing sparks the desire for curry as much as a few spicy appetizers served with tangy chutneys and relishes. Nibbles such as pakoras, samosas or onion bhajiyas whet the appetite, and when enjoyed with pickles and chutneys there is no limit to the taste sensations that will be experienced. Coconut Chutney, Mango Chutney and Lime Pickle offer a perfect balance of hot, sweet and sour flavours.

Coconut chutney

In traditional Tamil Nadu style, this chutney is fiery hot. Through the pungency of the chillies, you can savour the wonderful flavour and mellow taste, with the sweet undertone of coconut and the distinctive tang of tamarind. Desiccated coconut is used here, but by all means use fresh coconut if you prefer. It can be frozen in small portions for about 3 months.

SERVES 4–5

75g/3oz/1 cup desiccated (dry
    unsweetened shredded) coconut
1–2 green chillies, chopped (seeded
    if you like)
2.5ml/¹/₂ tsp salt or to taste
2.5ml/¹/₂ tsp sugar
15ml/1 tbsp natural (plain) yogurt
1cm/¹/₂in piece of fresh root ginger,
    roughly chopped
25ml/1¹/₂ tbsp tamarind juice or lime juice
15ml/1 tbsp sunflower oil or plain olive oil
2.5ml/¹/₂ tsp black mustard seeds
6–8 curry leaves
1 dried red chilli, chopped

1 Put the coconut in a bowl and pour in enough boiling water to just cover it. Set aside for 15–20 minutes, then put into a blender.

2 Add the green chillies, salt, sugar, yogurt, ginger and tamarind or lime juice. Blend until the ingredients are well mixed to a smooth purée and transfer the mixture to a serving bowl.

3 Heat the oil in a small wok or a steel ladle over a medium heat. When hot, but not smoking, add the mustard seeds, followed by the curry leaves and red chilli. Allow the seeds to crackle and the chilli to blacken slightly, then switch off the heat. Pour the entire mixture over the chutney. Mix well and serve at room temperature.

Nutritional information per portion: Energy 133kcal/548kJ; Protein 1.9g; Carbohydrate 4.1g, of which sugars 2g; Fat 12.3g, of which saturates 8.4g; Cholesterol 0mg; Calcium 20mg; Fibre 2.1g; Sodium 9mg.

Roasted tomato chutney

This chutney recipe comes from Darjeeling, with definite influences from Nepal. The Nepalese would roast the tomatoes over a wood fire to impart an unforgettable flavour. The tomatoes can be cooked on a barbecue then mixed with chillies, ginger, garlic and fresh coriander and made into a purée. This chutney is eaten fresh, although it will keep in the refrigerator for one week.

MAKES 225G/8OZ

700g/1½lb ripe tomatoes, halved

30ml/2 tbsp sunflower oil or plain olive oil

1–2 green chillies, chopped (seeded if you like)

1cm/½in piece of fresh root ginger, peeled and chopped

1 clove garlic, chopped

2 tbsp coriander (cilantro) leaves, chopped

½ tsp salt or to taste

1 Preheat the oven to 190°C/ 375°F/Gas 5. Put the tomato halves in a roasting pan and drizzle the oil over them. Roast in the centre of the oven for 20 minutes. Remove the tomatoes from the oven, leave them to cool and then peel off the skin.

2 Place the tomatoes in a blender or food processor with the remaining ingredients and purée until smooth. Store in a sterilized, airtight jar and keep in the refrigerator. Serve with all kinds of fried, grilled (broiled) and roasted appetizers, or use as a dip with bread or poppadums.

Nutritional information per portion: Energy 334kcal/1395kJ; Protein 6.4g; Carbohydrate 23.1g, of which sugars 22.8g; Fat 24.7g, of which saturates 3.3g; Cholesterol 0mg; Calcium 149mg; Fibre 9.5g; Sodium 80mg.

Mango chutney

Chutneys are prepared with fruits or vegetables, or both. Mango and tomato versions are made all over India, while herb chutneys are eaten in the north and west.

MAKES 450G/1LB/2 CUPS

3 firm green mangoes, cut into chunks
150ml/1/4 pint/2/3 cup cider vinegar
130g/41/2oz/2/3 cup light muscovado
    (brown) sugar
1 small fresh red chilli, split
2.5cm/1in piece fresh root ginger, grated
1 garlic clove, crushed
5 cardamom pods, bruised
2.5ml/1/2 tsp coriander seeds, crushed
1 bay leaf
2.5ml/1/2 tsp salt

1 Put the mango chunks into a pan, add the cider vinegar and cover. Cook over a low heat for 10 minutes, then stir in the remaining ingredients. Bring to the boil slowly, stirring.

2 Lower the heat and simmer gently for 30 minutes, until the mixture is syrupy. Leave to cool, then ladle into a hot sterilized jar and cover. Leave to rest for 1 week before serving.

Nutritional information per portion: Energy 1401kcal/5997kJ; Protein 8.7g; Carbohydrate 360.7g, of which sugars 356.6g; Fat 2.2g, of which saturates 0.9g; Cholesterol 0mg; Calcium 238mg; Fibre 27.8g; Sodium 1019mg.

COOK'S TIP
To sterilize jars for bottling pickles or chutneys, boil them in water for a minimum of 10 minutes. Chutneys that contain vinegar and sugar, such as this recipe for mango chutney, can be stored in the refrigerator for 3–6 months.

Lime pickle

Sharp lime pickle is one of the best-known Indian relishes. For this popular recipe, you will need ripe limes, with a yellow tinge on the skin.

MAKES ABOUT 900G/2LB/ 4 CUPS

10–12 limes
15ml/1 tbsp salt
120ml/4fl oz/¹/₂ cup malt vinegar
250ml/8fl oz/1 cup vegetable oil
5ml/1 tsp asafoetida
10–12 garlic cloves, crushed
**2.5cm/1in piece of fresh root
   ginger, grated**
10–12 curry leaves
**30ml/2 tbsp black mustard seeds,
   finely ground**
15ml/1 tbsp cumin seeds, finely ground
**10ml/2 tsp fenugreek seeds,
   finely ground**
10ml/2 tsp ground turmeric
10ml/2 tsp chilli powder
10 green chillies, halved
20ml/4 tsp salt
20ml/4 tsp sugar

1 Wash the limes and dry them with a cloth. Trim them, then cut them into quarters. Sprinkle the quarters with the salt and put them in a colander over a bowl. Set aside for 2 hours, then transfer them to another bowl and add the vinegar. Stir until any salt is dissolved and drain in the colander again.

2 Heat the oil in a pan over a medium heat and add the asafoetida, followed by the garlic, ginger and curry leaves. Allow them to brown in the pan slightly.

3 Add the ground seeds, turmeric and chilli powder, and stir-fry for 1 minute, then add the green chillies, salt and sugar. Stir-fry for 1 minute longer before adding the limes. Remove from the heat and allow to cool completely.

4 Store the lime pickle in sterilized, airtight jars. Leave the pickle in the jar for 4–5 weeks to mature before eating. The pickle will keep for around 10–12 months.

Nutritional information per portion: Energy 120kcal/492kJ; Protein 0.1g; Carbohydrate 0.3g, of which sugars 0.2g; Fat 13.1g, of which saturates 1.6g; Cholesterol 0mg; Calcium 9mg; Fibre 0.1g; Sodium 436mg.

Tomato and onion salad

This refreshing, tangy salad is an ideal side dish to serve with a curry. Raw vegetable salads are known as cachumbers *and are often served as side dishes, or before a main meal as part of a selection of poppadums, chutneys and relishes.*

SERVES 4–6

2 limes
2.5ml/¹/₂ tsp granulated (white) sugar
a few fresh coriander (cilantro) sprigs,
   chopped, plus extra for garnishing
2 onions, finely chopped
4 firm tomatoes, finely chopped
¹/₂ cucumber, finely chopped
1 fresh green chilli, finely chopped
salt and ground black pepper
a few fresh mint sprigs, to garnish

1 Extract the juice of the limes into a small bowl. Add the sugar, salt and pepper and allow to rest until the sugar and salt have competely dissolved. Mix together well.

2 Add the remaining ingredients and mix well. Chill, and garnish with fresh coriander and mint sprigs before serving.

Nutritional information per portion: Energy 42Kcal/176kJ; Protein 2g; Carbohydrate 8g, of which sugars 7g; Fat 1g, of which saturates 0g; Cholesterol 0mg; Calcium 31mg; Fibre 1.7g; Sodium 100mg.

Cucumber raita

Raitas are slightly sour, yogurt-based accompaniments that have a cooling effect on the palate when eaten with spicy foods. They help to balance out the flavours of an Indian meal. This is the cucumber version, which is one of the most popular varieties.

**MAKES ABOUT 600ML/
1 PINT/2¹/₂ CUPS**

¹/₂ cucumber
1 fresh green chilli, seeded and chopped
300ml/¹/₂ pint/1¹/₄ cups natural
　(plain) yogurt
1.5ml/¹/₄ tsp salt
1.5ml/¹/₄ tsp ground cumin

1 Dice the cucumber finely and place in a large mixing bowl. Sprinkle over the chopped green chilli and mix well to combine it with the cucumber.

2 Place the natural yogurt in a bowl and beat it with a fork until it becomes smooth, then stir it into the cucumber and chilli mixture in the large bowl.

3 Stir the salt and ground cumin into the yogurt mixture. Cover the bowl with clear film (plastic wrap) and chill in the refrigerator for at least 30 minutes before serving.

Nutritional information per portion: Energy 31kcal/131kJ; Protein 2.8g; Carbohydrate 4.2g, of which sugars 4g; Fat 0.6g, of which saturates 0.3g; Cholesterol 1mg; Calcium 104mg; Fibre 0.2g; Sodium 141mg.

Aubergine pickle

In this recipe, the moisture from the vegetable must be extracted before preserving in the spice-perfumed oil. The pickle is delicious served with snacks such as poppadums.

**MAKES 350–400G/
12–14OZ PICKLE**

1 large aubergine (eggplant), approx
    400g/14oz, peeled and diced
15ml/1 tbsp salt
120ml/4fl oz/¹/₂ cup vegetable oil
2.5ml/¹/₂ tsp ground asafoetida
10 garlic cloves, crushed
5cm/2in piece of fresh root ginger, grated
5ml/1 tsp mustard seeds
5ml/1 tsp fenugreek seeds
7.5ml/1¹/₂ tsp cumin seeds
25g/1oz/2 tbsp granulated (white) sugar
30ml/2 tbsp salt
175ml/6fl oz/³/₄ cup white wine vinegar

1 Cube the aubergine and then sprinkle the chunks with salt and mix well. Put them in muslin (cheesecloth), tie it up, and place in a colander over a bowl. Put a clean weight directly on top and leave to drain off all the water. This will take aproximately 6–7 hours.

2 Heat the vegetable oil over a medium heat and add the asafoetida, followed by the garlic and ginger. Stir-fry for about 1 minute.

3 Grind the mustard, fenugreek and cumin seeds finely in a coffee grinder or blender. Add the ground ingredients to the pan and fry for 2 minutes. Next, add the sugar, salt, vinegar and aubergine chunks. Stir, then simmer gently for 20–25 minutes or until the aubergine is tender. Cool completely and store in a sterilized jar. Allow 12–14 days for the pickle to mature, then serve as a condiment alongside Indian snacks and curries.

Nutritional information per portion: Energy 870kcal/3609kJ; Protein 9.1g; Carbohydrate 46.7g, of which sugars 34.8g; Fat 73.7g, of which saturates 8g; Cholesterol 0mg; Calcium 89mg; Fibre 9.6g; Sodium 3946mg.

Onion, mango and peanut chaat

Chaats are spiced relishes of vegetables and nuts served with Indian meals. Amchur adds a deliciously fruity sourness to this mixture of onions and mango.

SERVES 4

90g/3½oz/scant 1 cup unsalted peanuts
15ml/1 tbsp groundnut (peanut) oil
1 onion, chopped
10cm/4in piece cucumber, seeded and cut
    into 5mm/¼in dice
1 mango, peeled, stoned (pitted)
    and diced
1 green chilli, seeded and chopped
30ml/2 tbsp chopped fresh
    coriander (cilantro)
15ml/1 tbsp chopped fresh mint
15ml/1 tbsp lime juice, or to taste
light muscovado (brown) sugar, to taste

FOR THE CHAAT MASALA

10ml/2 tsp ground toasted cumin seeds
2.5ml/½ tsp cayenne pepper
5ml/1 tsp mango powder (amchur)
2.5ml/½ tsp garam masala
pinch of ground asafoetida
salt and ground black pepper

1 To make the chaat masala, mix all the spices together, then season with 2.5ml/½ tsp each of salt and pepper.

2 Fry the peanuts in the oil until lightly browned, stirring frequently, then drain on kitchen paper until cool.

3 Put the onion in a mixing bowl with the cucumber, mango, chilli, fresh coriander and mint. Sprinkle in 5ml/1 tsp of the chaat masala and mix well to thoroughly combine.

4 Stir in the peanuts and then add lime juice and/or sugar to taste. Set the mixture aside for 20–30 minutes to give the flavours time to develop. Transfer the mixture into a serving bowl, sprinkle another 5ml/1 tsp of the chaat masala over the top and serve immediately.

Nutritional information per portion: Energy 189kcal/788kJ; Protein 6.9g; Carbohydrate 9.8g, of which sugars 6.6g; Fat 14g, of which saturates 2.4g; Cholesterol 0mg; Calcium 41mg; Fibre 2.4g; Sodium 4mg.

Curry Basics

The secret of making authentic curries

is in the combination and judicious use

of aromatic spices, the freshest herbs,

garlic and ginger, and of course

chillies. This section outlines the

ingredients you will need, how to make

your own curry powders and pastes,

and tips on storage and dry-frying

seeds, as well as the lowdown on rice

and breads, which are essential sides to

serve with your curries.

Aromatics, spices and herbs

Spices are integral to both the flavour and aroma of a dish. Some spices are used for the taste they impart, while other spices, known as aromatics, are used for their aroma. One spice can alter the taste of a dish and a mixture will also affect its colour and texture.

The quantities of spices and salt specified in recipes are measured, but you may prefer to add more or less. This is especially true of fresh chillies and chilli powder.

Fresh and dried herbs are also important for their colour, flavour, aroma and texture in a curry. Because they need little cooking, they retain an intensity of flavour and fragrance.

Ginger

Fresh root ginger is an important ingredient in many Indian curries. Its refreshing citrus flavour is pleasantly sharp. The root should be plump with a fairly smooth skin, which is peeled off. Young root ginger is mild; older roots have a more pungent flavour. The flavour of dried powdered ginger is not so strong and It is often added to curry powder.

Garlic

Available fresh and dried, garlic is used for its strong, aromatic flavour, and is used with ginger in curries.

BELOW: *Fresh root ginger*

BELOW: *Ground ginger*

Pulping garlic

Fresh garlic is used so often in curries that it is practical to prepare it in bulk and store in the refrigerator or freezer until needed.

Separate the garlic bulb into cloves and peel off the papery skin. Process the whole cloves in a food processor until smooth. Freeze the pulp in ice-cube trays. Put 5ml/1 tsp in each compartment, freeze, remove from the tray and store in the freezer in a sealed plastic bag. Or, store in an airtight container in the refrigerator for 3–4 weeks.

Preparing fresh root ginger

Fresh root ginger has a clean, pungent taste. It is widely available from supermarkets and markets.

To grate ginger, remove the skin using a sharp knife or vegetable peeler, then grate the ginger using the fine side of a metal cheese grater. To chop, slice into fine strips, then chop as required.

Pulping fresh roor ginger

Pulped fresh root ginger is time-consuming to prepare. Instead, prepare a large quantity and store in the freezer until needed.

Peel off the outer skin. Roughly chop, then process in a food processor, adding a little water to get a smooth consistency. Store the pulp in the refrigerator for 3–4 weeks or freeze in ice-cube trays used for the purpose.

Chillies

These hot peppers belong to the genus capsicum, along with sweet (bell) peppers. Some varieties are extremely fiery and all chillies should be used with caution. Much of the severe heat of fresh chillies is contained in the seeds, and the heat can be toned down by removing these before use. Like other spicy foods, chillies are perfect for hot climates as they cause blood to rush to the surface of the skin, promoting instant cooling.

Chillies vary in size and colour, but as a rule, dark green chillies tend to be hotter than light green ones. Red chillies are usually hotter still, and some will darken to brown or black

Preparing dried chillies

Dried chillies are available from supermarkets and Indian food stores. To prepare chillies, remove the stems and seeds, then break each chilli into two or three pieces. Put the pieces in a small bowl and cover with hot water. Leave to stand for 30 minutes, then drain. Use the chilli pieces as they are, or chop them finely.

LEFT: *Green and red bird's eye chillies*

when fully ripe. Shape and colour give no sure indication of the hotness, and it is wise to be wary of any unfamiliar variety. Dried chillies can be used whole or coarsely crushed.

Chilli powder is a fiery ground spice that should be used with great caution. The heat varies from brand to brand, so adjust quantities to suit your taste buds. Some brands include other spices and herbs, as well as ground chillies, and these may not be appropriate to the dish you are cooking, so check the label carefully.

Watchpoint

All chillies contain capsaicin, an oily substance, that can cause intense irritation to sensitive skin. If you get capsaicin on your hands and transfer it to your eyes, it will be very painful. Wash hands with soapy water after handling. Dry your hands and rub a little oil into the skin to remove any stinging juices. Many cooks prefer to wear rubber (latex) gloves.

BELOW: *The colour of chillies gives no sure indication of hotness, although red chillies are usually hotter.*

Preparing fresh chillies

Using two or more fresh chillies will make a dish quite hot. If you prefer a milder flavour, reduce the amount of chilli used, and remove the seeds and pithy membrane.

1 Cut the chillies in half lengthways. Remove the membranes and seeds.

2 Cut the chilli flesh lengthways into long, thin strips.

3 Cut the strips of chilli into tiny dice.

Aniseed

These liquorice-flavoured seeds are used in many fried and deep-fried Indian dishes as an aid to digestion.

Cinnamon

One of the earliest known spices, cinnamon has a highly aromatic, sweet, warm flavour. It is sold ready-ground and as sticks, which are quill-like shapes rolled from the bark of the cinnamon tree. Use cinnamon sticks whole or broken, as directed in individual recipes, and remove them from the food before serving. Ground cinnamon is a useful pantry staple.

Cloves

Originally found in the Spice Islands of Indonesia, cloves were taken to the Seychelles and Mauritius early in the 18th century. Cloves are the unopened flower buds of a tree that belongs to the myrtle family. They have an aromatic and sometimes fiery flavour and an intense fragrance, and are used to flavour many sweet and savoury dishes. Cloves are usually added whole to recipes. Their warm flavour complements all rich meats, and they need no preparation.

are one of the ingredients added to spice mixtures.

Cumin

White cumin seeds are oval, ridged and greenish brown in colour. They have a strong aroma and flavour and can be used whole or ground. Ready-ground cumin powder is widely available, but it should be bought in small quantities as it loses its flavour rapidly. Black cumin seeds are dark and aromatic. They are one of the ingredients used to make garam masala, and can be used to flavour curries and rice.

Turmeric

A member of the ginger family but without ginger's characteristic heat, turmeric is a rhizome that is indigenous to Asia. Turmeric shares saffron's ability to colour food yellow, although its flavour lacks the

LEFT: *Ground and fresh turmeric*

BELOW: *From left, cloves, ground cinnamon, and cinnamon sticks*

ABOVE: *From left, cumin seeds, fenugreek and ground cumin*

Ground cloves

subtlety of saffron. Fresh turmeric adds a warm and slightly musky flavour to food, but it has a strong, bitter flavour and should be used sparingly. Turmeric has a natural affinity with fish, and is also used in rice, dhal and vegetable dishes.

Dhana jeera powder

This commonly used spice mixture is made from ground roasted coriander and cumin seeds. The proportions are generally two parts coriander to one part cumin. It is used in fairly large quantities to flavour curries.

Fennel seeds

Similar in appearance to cumin, fennel seeds have a sweet taste and are used to flavour curries. They can be chewed as a mouth-freshener after a spicy meal.

Mustard seeds

Whole black and brown mustard seeds are indigenous to India and appear often in Indian cooking. The seeds have no aroma in their raw state, but when roasted or fried in ghee or hot oil they release a rich, nutty flavour and aroma. Mustard seeds are commonly used with vegetables and dhal dishes.

Nigella seeds

This spice has a sharp and tingling taste. Its aroma is released on heating and it is frequently used in Indian vegetarian dishes.

Dry-frying mustard seeds

Mustard seeds release their aroma when heated so should be dry-fried before they are added to a dish.

Heat a little ghee or vegetable oil in a wok, karahi or large pan, and add the mustard seeds. Shake the pan over the heat until the seeds start to change colour. Stir the seeds from time to time. Use the pan lid to stop the seeds jumping out of the pan when they start to splutter and pop.

ABOVE: *Small green cardamom pods and the larger brown variety*

Onion seeds

Black, triangular shaped and aromatic, onion seeds are used in pickles and to flavour vegetable curries and lentil dishes.

Garam masala

This is a mixture of spices that can be made at home from freshly ground spices, or purchased ready-made. There is no set recipe, but a typical mixture might include black cumin seeds, peppercorns, cloves, cinnamon and black cardamom pods. Many variations on garam masala are sold commercially, as pastes ready-made in jars. These can be subtituted for garam masala, and will make useful pantry standbys.

Asafoetida

This seasoning is a resin with an acrid and very bitter taste and a strong odour. It is used primarily as an anti-flatulent, and only minute quantities are used in recipes. Store in a glass jar with a strong airtight seal to prevent the smell dispersing into other ingredients in the pantry.

Cardamom pods

This spice is native to India, where it is considered the most prized spice after saffron. The pods can be used whole or the husks can be removed to release the seeds; whole pods should be always removed from the dish before serving. They have a slightly pungent, but very aromatic taste. They come in three varieties: green, white and black or brown. The green and white pods can be used for both sweet and savoury dishes or to flavour rice. Black or brown pods are used only for savoury dishes.

Nutmeg

Whole nutmeg should be grated on a special nutmeg grater to release its sweet, nutty flavour. Grated nutmeg imparts a similar, though less intense, flavour, and makes a very useful pantry standby.

ABOVE: *Whole nutmeg and grated nutmeg*

RIGHT: *From left, white, black and pink peppercorns*

RIGHT: *From left, saffron powder and threads*

Peppercorns

Black peppercorns are native to India, and are a key ingredient in garam masala. White peppercorns are less aromatic, and the pink variety is mildly toxic so only small amounts are used. Peppercorns are used whole or ground, and the black variety has the strongest taste.

Paprika

A mild, sweet red powder, paprika is often used in place of or alongside chillies in westernized Indian cooking to add colour to a dish.

ABOVE: *Paprika*

Saffron

The dried stigmas of the saffron crocus, which is native to Asia Minor, is the world's most expensive spice. To produce 450g/1lb of saffron requires 60,000 stigmas, but fortunately, only a small quantity is required to flavour and colour a dish. Saffron is sold as threads and as a powder.

Curry leaves

Bright green and shiny, curry leaves are similar in appearance to bay leaves, but they have a different flavour. The leaves of a hardwood tree that is indigenous to India, they are widely used in India cooking, and in Sri Lanka. Curry leaves have a warm fragrance with a subtle hint of sweet, green pepper or tangerine. They release their full flavour when bruised, and impart a highly distinctive flavour to curries.

ABOVE: *Dried curry leaves*

Curry leaves are sold dried and occasionally fresh in Indian food stores. Fresh leaves freeze well, but the dried leaves make a poor substitute, as they become brittle and rapidly lose their fragrance.

Bay leaves

Indian bay leaves come from the cassia tree, which is similar to the tree from which cinnamon is taken. Bay leaves sold in the West are taken from the laurel tree. When used fresh, bay leaves have a deliciously sweet flavour, but they keep well in dried form, if stored in a cool, dark place in an airtight jar. Bay leaves are used in meat and rice dishes.

Coriander

There is no substitute for fresh coriander (cilantro), and the more that is used in Indian cooking the better. Coriander imparts a wonderful aroma and flavour, and is used both as an ingredient in cooking, and sprinkled over dishes as a garnish. Chopped coriander can be frozen successfully; the frozen coriander does not need to be defrosted before

BELOW: *Bay leaves*

BELOW: *Fresh coriander (cilantro)*

unpleasant bitterness to a dish if used. Fenugreek seeds are flat, extremely pungent and slightly bitter. They only appear in a few recipes, where they are added whole, mainly for taste; these should be used cautiously. Dried fenugreek leaves are sold in Indian food stores. Store them in an airtight jar, in a cool, dark place; they will keep for about 12 months. Fenugreek seeds are small and pungent, and are widely used in spice mixtures.

use. Coriander seeds and ground coriander powder are used for flavouring. The seeds have a pungent, slightly lemony flavour, and are used coarsely ground in meat, fish and poultry dishes. Ground coriander, which is a brownish powder, is an important constituent of any curry spice mixture.

Mint

There are many varieties of mint available, and the stronger-flavoured types tend to be used in Indian cooking. These taste slightly sweet and have a cool aftertaste. Mint has a fresh, stimulating aroma and is traditionally used with lamb, as well as for flavouring some vegetables, and for making chutneys and refreshing raitas. Mint is added at the end of cooking time, in order to retain the flavour.

Fenugreek

Fresh fenugreek is generally sold in bunches. It has very small leaves and is used to flavour meat and vegetarian dishes. Always discard the stalks, which will impart an

RIGHT: *Aromatic fresh fenugreek leaves are widely used in savoury Indian dishes. The stalks are usually discarded.*

Freezing fresh coriander

Fresh coriander (cilantro) is widely used in curries owing to its flavour and aroma. Buy bunches and freeze any that is not required.

1 Cut off the roots and any thick stalks, retaining the fine stalks.

2 Wash the leaves in cold water and leave in a strainer to drain.

3 Chop the leaves and store small amounts in plastic bags in the freezer.

Curry powders and pastes

Powders and pastes are blends of spices, chillies and herbs that are used as the basis of a curry. Spices can be blended as needed, but for convenience you can prepare a quantity in advance.

Curry powder

This basic recipe for a dry spice blend is mild, but you can increase the quantity of dried chilli if you prefer a hotter curry.

Makes about 115g/4oz/¹⁄₂ cup

50g/2oz/¹⁄₂ cup coriander seeds
60ml/4 tbsp cumin seeds
30ml/2 tbsp fennel seeds
30ml/2 tbsp fenugreek seeds
4 dried red chillies
5 curry leaves
15ml/1 tbsp chilli powder
15ml/1 tbsp ground turmeric
2.5ml/¹⁄₂ tsp salt

1 Dry-roast the whole spices in a wok, karahi or large pan for 8–10 minutes, shaking the pan until the spices darken and release a rich aroma. Allow to cool.

2 Put the dry-roasted whole spices in a spice mill and grind to a fine powder.

3 Add the ground, roasted spices to the chilli powder, turmeric and salt in a large glass bowl and mix well. Store the curry powder in an airtight container.

Garam masala

Garam means hot and masala means spices. It is used mainly for meat, although it can be used in poultry and rice dishes. The aroma is too strong for fish or vegetable dishes.

Makes about 50g/2oz/¹⁄₄ cup

10 dried red chillies
3 x 2.5cm/1in pieces cinnamon stick
2 curry leaves
30ml/2 tbsp coriander seeds
30ml/2 tbsp cumin seeds
5ml/1 tsp black peppercorns
5ml/1 tsp cloves
5ml/1 tsp fenugreek seeds
5ml/1 tsp black mustard seeds
1.5ml/¹⁄₄ tsp chilli powder

1 Dry-roast the whole dried red chillies, cinnamon sticks and curry leaves in a wok, karahi or large pan over a low heat for about 2 minutes.

2 Add the coriander and cumin seeds, black peppercorns, cloves, fenugreek and mustard seeds, and dry-roast for 8–10 minutes, shaking the pan from side to side until the spices begin to darken in colour and release a rich aroma. Allow the mixture to cool.

3 Using either a spice mill or a stainless steel mortar and pestle, grind the roasted spices to a fine powder.

4 Transfer the powder to a glass bowl and mix in the chilli powder. Store the garam masala in an airtight container such as a jar.

Cook's Tip

Both the curry powder and the garam masala will keep for 2–4 months in an airtight container in a cool, dark place. Once opened, store in the refrigerator.

Curry paste

A curry paste is a wet blend of spices, herbs and chillies cooked with oil and vinegar, which help to preserve the spices during storage. It is a quick and convenient way of adding a spice mixture to a curry, and different blends will produce different flavours. Store in the refrigerator.

Makes about 600ml/1 pint/2½ cups

50g/2oz/½ cup coriander seeds
60ml/4 tbsp cumin seeds
30ml/2 tbsp fennel seeds
30ml/2 tbsp fenugreek seeds
4 dried red chillies
5 curry leaves
15ml/1 tbsp chilli powder
15ml/1 tbsp ground turmeric
150ml/¼ pint/⅔ cup wine vinegar
250ml/8fl oz/1 cup vegetable oil

1 Grind the whole spices to a powder in a spice mill. Transfer to a bowl and add the remaining ground spices.

2 Mix the spices until blended. Add the wine vinegar and stir. Add 75ml/5 tbsp water and mix to a paste.

Cook's tip

Curry pastes will keep for 3–4 weeks after opening, in the refrigerator.

3 Heat the oil in a large pan and stir-fry the spice paste for 10 minutes, or until all the water has been absorbed. When the oil rises to the surface the paste is cooked. Cool slightly before spooning the paste into airtight jars.

Tikka paste

This is a delicious, versatile paste with a slightly sour flavour.

Makes about 475ml/16fl oz/2 cups

30ml/2 tbsp each coriander and cumin seeds
25ml/1½ tbsp garlic powder
30ml/2 tbsp paprika
15ml/1 tbsp garam masala
15ml/1 tbsp ground ginger
10ml/2 tsp chilli powder
2.5ml/½ tsp ground turmeric
15ml/1 tbsp dried mint
1.5ml/¼ tsp salt
5ml/1 tsp lemon juice
a few drops of red and yellow food colouring
150ml/¼ pint/⅔ cup wine vinegar
150ml/¼ pint/⅔ cup vegetable oil

1 Grind the coriander and cumin seeds to a fine powder using a spice mill or mortar and pestle. Spoon the mixture into a bowl and add the remaining spices, the mint and salt, stirring well.

2 Mix the spice powder with the lemon juice, food colourings and wine vinegar and add 30ml/2 tbsp water to form a thin paste.

3 Heat the oil in a large pan and stir-fry the paste for 10 minutes, until all the water has been absorbed. When the oil rises to the surface, the paste is cooked. Cool then spoon into jars.

Cook's Tip

Heat a little more oil and pour on top of the paste in an airtight jar. This will help to preserve the paste and stop any mould from forming during storage. Store in the refrigerator.

Rice

This staple grain is often served with almost every meal in some parts of India, and there are many ways of cooking it. Plain boiled rice is an everyday accompaniment; for special occasions, it is often combined with other ingredients.

There is no definitive way to cook plain rice, but whatever the recipe, the aim is to produce dry, separate-grained rice that is cooked through yet still retains some bite. The secret is the amount of water added: the rice must be able to absorb it all.

Basmati rice
Known as the prince of rices, basmati is the recommended rice for Indian curries – not only because it is easy to cook and produces an excellent finished result, but because it has a cooling effect on hot and spicy curries. Basmati is a slender, long grain, milled rice grown in northern India, the Punjab, parts of Pakistan and in the foothills of the Himalayas. Its name means fragrant, and it has a distinctive and appealing aroma. After harvesting it is aged for a year, which gives it the characteristic flavour and a light, fluffy texture. Basmati can be used in almost any savoury dish, particularly curries or pilaus, and is the essential ingredient in biryanis. White and brown basmati rices are widely available from supermarkets and Indian food stores.

Patna rice
This rice takes its name from Patna in eastern India. At one time, most of the long grain rice sold in Europe came from Patna, and the term was used loosely to mean any long grain rice, whatever its origin. The custom still persists in parts of the United States, but elsewhere Patna is used to describe the specific variety of rice grown in the eastern state of Bihar. Patna rice is used in the same way as other long grain rices, and is suitable when plain boiled rice is called for.

BELOW: *Patna rice, a long grain rice native to eastern India.*

ABOVE: *White basmati, probably the most commonly eaten rice in India.*

Cooking plain boiled rice
Always make sure you use a tight-fitting lid for your rice pan. If you do not have a lid that fits tightly, you can either wrap a dishtowel around the lid or put some foil between the lid and the pan to make a snug fit. Try not to remove the lid until the rice is cooked. (The advantage of using just a lid is that you can tell when the rice is ready because steam begins to escape, visibly and rapidly.)

As a rough guide, allow 75g/3oz/ scant ½ cup rice per person.

1 Put the dry rice in a colander and rinse it under cold running water until the water runs clear.

2 Place the rice in a large, deep pan and pour in enough cold water to come 2cm/¾in above the surface of the rice. Add a pinch of salt and, if you like, 5ml/1 tsp vegetable oil, stir once and bring to the boil.

3 Stir once more, reduce the heat to the lowest possible setting and cover the pan with a tight-fitting lid.

4 Cook the rice for 12–15 minutes, then turn off the heat and leave the rice to stand, still tightly covered, for about 10 minutes.

5 Before serving, gently fluff up the rice with a fork or slotted rice spoon – the slotted spoon will prevent you from breaking up the grains, which would make the rice mushy.

Breads

A wide variety of flatbreads are essential fare to serve with curries. Most traditional breads are unleavened, that is, made without any raising agent, and are made with wholemeal (whole-wheat) flour, known as chapati flour or atta.

Some breads are cooked dry on a hot griddle, some are fried with a little oil, and others are deep-fried to make savoury puffs. To enjoy Indian breads at their best they should be eaten hot.

Naan

Probably the most well-known Indian bread, naan is made with plain (all-purpose) flour, yogurt and yeast. Some contemporary recipes favour the use of a chemical raising agent such as bicarbonate of soda (baking soda) or self-raising (self-rising) flour as a leaven in place of yeast. The yogurt is important for the fermentation of the dough, and some naan are made entirely using a yogurt fermentation, which gives the bread its light, puffy texture and soft crust.

The flavour comes partly from the soured yogurt and partly from the tandoor, which is the the clay oven, sunk into the ground, in which the bread is cooked. The dough is flattened against the hot walls of the oven and the pull of gravity produces the characteristic teardrop shape. As the dough scorches and puffs up, it produces a bread that is soft and crisp. Naan can be eaten with most meat or vegetable dishes. Many types of flavoured naan are available, including plain, coriander (cilantro) and garlic, and masala naan.

Chapatis

The favourite bread of central and southern India is the chapati, a thin, flat, unleavened bread made from ground wholemeal flour. Chapatis are cooked on a hot tava, a concave-shaped Indian griddle. Chapatis have a light texture and fairly bland flavour, which makes them an ideal accompaniment for highly spiced curry dishes.

Rotis

There are many variations of chapatis, including rotis and dana rotis. These are unleavened breads, made using chapati flour to which ghee, oil, and/or fresh coriander are added. They are rolled out thinly and cooked like chapatis.

Parathas

A paratha is similar to a chapati except that it contains ghee

ABOVE: *Poppadums*

(clarified butter), to give a richer flavour and flakier texture. Parathas are much thicker than chapatis and are shallow-fried. Plain parathas can be stuffed with various fillings, such as spiced potato. Stuffed parathas are served as a snack.

Pooris

Another popular variation on the chapati is the poori, which is a small, deep-fried puffy bread made from chapati flour. Pooris are eaten sizzling hot and are often served for breakfast. They can be plain or flavoured with cumin, turmeric and chilli powder, which are mixed into the dough. Pooris are often served with fish or vegetable curries.

Poppadums

These are large, thin crisp disks, which can be bought ready-cooked or ready-to-cook. In India they are sold in markets, and are available plain or flavoured with spices or pepper. The dough is generally made from dried beans, but can also be made from potatoes or sago. It is thinly rolled and left to dry in the sun. Poppadums are cooked either by deep-frying or placing under a hot grill (broiler).

RIGHT:
Naan

Index